Analysis Of The Human Rights Impact Of Estate Regeneration In the United Kingdom

Shemi Esquire

CW00868467

Table of contents:

Shemi Esquire ©June 2022

Analysis Of The Human Rights Impact Of Estate Regeneration In the United Kingdom

Shemi Esquire

Abstract

This text evaluates the consequences of housing estate regeneration on residents and communities, in the framework of the ECHR. The essay places significant emphasis on *art 6, 8 and Article 1 of the 1st protocol.*[1]

Broadly, the case for and against estate regeneration is a ferociously contested one. Advocates of estate regeneration contend that housing estate regeneration, is beneficial to communities and residents. They assert that housing estate regeneration leads to job creation, allows the rejuvenation of living spaces and increases the supply of *social and affordable* housing.[2]

However, residents and activists, argue that the practice leads to displacement, dispossession and disenfranchisement of residents.[3] Further stating that the practice is a form of psychological violence, inflicted on disproportionately, racially diverse and historically disadvantaged communities.[4]

Further observations from opponents of estate regeneration, suggest that the outcomes of housing estate regeneration, are arguably associated with commercial

---

[1] Grabenwarter, Christoph. *"European Convention on Human Rights." European Convention on Human Rights. Nomos Verlagsgesellschaft mbH & Co. KG, 2014.*

[2] *Adonis, Andrew, and B. Davies. "City villages: More homes, better communities." CITY VILLAGES (2015): 5.*

[3] *Potent Whisper,No-other-option-than-estate-regeneration-we-beg-to-differ, /https://www.egi.co.uk/2017*

[44] *Perera, Jessica. "The London clearances: Race, housing and policing." London, UK: The Institute of Race Relations (2019*

interests,[5] that lead to negative outcomes for residents and communities. Thereby potentially heightening the intergenerational inequality, which was aggravated by the impact of covid19 from 2020 to date.[6]

Introduction

As indicated above, this text evaluates the effect of estate regeneration[7] on residents and other applicable affected parties, from the viewpoint of the ECHR. The analysis specifically discusses public authorities' practices, by scrutinising the causal practical policies, decisions and the impact thereof on residents.[8]

The text starts by providing an overview of estate regeneration and compulsory purchase orders, then proceeds to examine the sources of CPO legal powers and the consequential detrimental impact, in a human rights framework.

In the closing sections, the text explores whether the contemporary CPO legal framework, practically safeguards the overall socio-economic interests and wellbeing of residents, then concludes by suggesting recommendations for review of the CPO process.[9]

---

[5] Hodkinson, Stuart. "Housing regeneration and the private finance initiative in England: Unstitching the neoliberal urban straitjacket." Antipode 43.2 (2011): 358-383.

[6] Elliott-Cooper, Adam, Phil Hubbard, and Loretta Lees. "Moving beyond Marcuse: Gentrification, displacement and the violence of un-homing." Progress in Human Geography 44.3 (2020): 492-509.; Shemi Esquire, The Rich Have Lawyers, The London Takings, 2020.
Shemi Esquire, The compatibility of compulsory purchase orders with human rights,2019; Shemi Esquire, Human Rights and Housing Estate Regeneration, 2020.; Minton, Anna. "The price of regeneration." Places Journal (2018).; Dening, Geraldine, and Simon Elmer. The Costs of Estate Regeneration: A Report by Architects for Social Housing. 2018.

[7] Compulsory purchase orders, https://www.legislation.gov.uk/ukpga/1981/67/section/1

[88] Alice Delotti, Estate Regeneration and Community Impacts https://www.unicef.org/child-rights-conventionChallenges and lessons for social landlords, developers and local councils,2016.

[9] Shemi Esquire, The Rich Have Lawyers, The London Takings, 2020.

CPO Definition

Compulsory purchase orders, [10] are a legal mechanism deployed by acquiring authorities to compulsorily acquire land,[11] which may be occupied or encumbered with competing property or legal interests.[12]

CPOs *'require approval of a confirming minister under the Acquisition of Land Act 1981'.*[13] There are various *enabling powers* available and the determination to authorise CPOs, will partly depend on specific powers used.[14] CPOs can also be implemented through acquisition of the freehold which should be distinguished from requisition, which is a form of possession with interests, *'carved out of the estate'.*[15]

The acquiring authority does not have to use a CPO to achieve its objectives and can acquire the freehold or let the leasehold expire.[16] Hence, a CPO is practically a form of imposed compensation on the landowner, without considering the gain by the acquiring party.[17] In that context, it is a key theme of this analysis, that CPOs interfere

---

Shemi Esquire, The compatibility of compulsory purchase orders with human rights,2019; Shemi Esquire, Human Rights and Housing Estate Regeneration, 2020.
[10] *Compulsory purchase orders, https://www.legislation.gov.uk/ukpga/1981/67/section/1*
[11] */Knock It Down or Do It Up pdf, https://www.london.gov.uk*
[12] *1 https://www.legislation.gov.uk/*
[13] *F-Gidance-on-compulsory-purchase-and-the-crichel-down-rules-for-the-disposal-of-surplus-land-.; Shemi Esquire, The Rich Have Lawyers, The London Takings, 2020.*
Shemi Esquire, The compatibility of compulsory purchase orders with human rights,2019; Shemi Esquire, Human Rights and Housing Estate Regeneration, 2020.

[14] *Such public bodies with statutory powers include 'local authorities national parks, some executive agencies, the Homes and Communities Agency, health service bodies and government ministers.'14*
[15] *Guy Roots, Michael Humphries, James Pereira, Robert Fookes The Law of Compulsory Purchase, pg. 13, 2011, 2nd Edition*
[16] *DCLG, Compulsory Purchase and Compensation to Residential Owners and Occupiers; Shemi Esquire, The Rich Have Lawyers, The London Takings, 2020;*
Shemi Esquire, The compatibility of compulsory purchase orders with human rights,2019; Shemi Esquire, Human Rights and Housing Estate Regeneration, 2020.

[17] *By Guy Roots, Michael Humphries, James Pereira, Robert Fookes The Law of Compulsory Purchase,*

with residents' human rights,[18] in the context of the regeneration of social housing estates.[19]

Such arguable human rights interference emanates from the fact that estate regeneration, through CPOs, is inherently coercive right from inception, especially that it is enabled and championed by aspects of the legal system.[20]

Effectively, residents choose between cooperating with the expropriation of their homes or face costly protracted legal and campaign battles, at the expense of their, well-being, [21] associated financial strain, displacement and related spiral consequences.

This is amplified by the fact that, from inception, the CPO process is presented by local authorities, as *simply a negotiation of the inevitable expropriating one's home*, a form of a fait accompli. This reflects the imbalance of power, the innate inequality and the physical as well as psychological compulsion that leads to displacement.[22]

Therefore, viewed from that perspective, there is an arguable case for such expropriation to be inherently indicative of infringement of human rights associated with a home, family life and the accompanying support networks. Such associated rights can be reflected in the framework of socioeconomic and political rights, that stem

---

[18] *Adélaïde Remiche, Yordanova and Others v Bulgaria: The Influence of the Social Right to Adequate Housing on the Interpretation of the Civil Right to Respect for One's Home, Human Rights Law Review, Volume 12, Issue 4, December 2012, Pages 787–800, https://doi.org/10.1093/hrlr/ngs033*

[19] *Hubbard P and Lees L, "The Right to Community?" (2018) 22 City 8*

[20] *Hodkinson, Stuart, and Chris Essen. "Grounding accumulation by dispossession in everyday life: The unjust geographies of urban regeneration under the private finance initiative." International Journal of Law in the Built Environment (2015).*

[21] *While the acquiring authorities, in this case local authorities are also the prosecuting authorities and planning adjudicators, with access to public resources to fund lawyers, architects, consultants and public relations firms.*

[22] *Dening, Geraldine, and Simon Elmer. The Costs of Estate Regeneration: A Report by Architects for Social Housing. 2018.*

from being rooted in a community with access to socio-economic opportunities.[23]This practice is particularly evident, in urban areas like London especially for racial minorities[24] who face historical inequalities and disadvantages. An issue that was reflected in *Adelaide Remiche, Yordanova and Others v Bulgaria,* where the court considered a complaint from the Roma community who were being expelled from their homes, built on municipal land.[25]the court concluded that expelling a community of several hundreds, had widespread ramifications, beyond losing a home.

It was further emphasised that *'having regard to the fact that the case concerns the expulsion of the applicants as part of a community of several hundred persons and that this measure could have repercussions on the applicants' lifestyle and social and family ties, it may be considered that the interference would affect not only their "homes", but also their "private and family life".[26] The Court must examine, therefore, whether such interference, if it materialises, would be lawful and necessary in a democratic society for the achievement of one or several of the legitimate aims set out in paragraph 2 of Article 8'.* Hence, enhancing the view, that estate expropriation, has wider associated detrimental effects, beyond property transactions.[27]

---

[23] Hearne, Rory, and Padraic Kenna. "Using the human rights-based approach to tackle housing deprivation in an Irish urban housing estate." Journal of Human Rights Practice 6.1 (2014): 1-25.; Hearne, Rory. "Realising the "right to the city": Developing a human rights-based framework for regeneration of areas of urban disadvantage." International Journal of Law in the Built Environment (2013).

[24] Perera, Jessica. "The London clearances: Race, housing and policing." London, UK: The Institute of Race Relations (2019). Elliott-Cooper, Adam, Phil Hubbard, and Loretta Lees. "Moving beyond Marcuse: Gentrification, displacement and the violence of un-homing." Progress in Human Geography 44.3 (2020): 492-509. ; Hubbard, Phil, and Loretta Lees. "The right to community? Legal geographies of resistance on London's gentrification frontiers." City 22.1 (2018): 8-25. Shemi Esquire, The Rich Have Lawyers, The London Takings, 2020;
Shemi Esquire, The compatibility of compulsory purchase orders with human rights,2019; Shemi Esquire, Human Rights and Housing Estate Regeneration, 2020.

[25] Adélaïde Remiche, Yordanova and Others v Bulgaria: The Influence of the Social Right to Adequate Housing on the Interpretation of the Civil Right to Respect for One's Home, Human Rights Law Review, Volume 12, Issue 4, December 2012, Pages 787–800, https://doi.org/10.1093/hrlr/ngs033

[26] (see, similarly, Chapman v. the United Kingdom [GC], no. 27238/95, § 73, ECHR 2001 I).

[27]Dixon, Tim, et al. "Measuring the initial social sustainability impacts of estate regeneration: a case study of Acton Gardens, London." Journal of Sustainability Research 1.1 (2019).Shemi Esquire, The Rich Have Lawyers, The London Takings, 2020.

Shemi Esquire

For a holistic understanding of estate regeneration, it is imperative to examine, CPO sources of powers and jurisdiction, which are briefly examined below.

CPO Jurisdiction

Parliament legislated for the legal taking of property in the interests of the public good and requires a specified legislated process, [28] under compulsory purchase procedures.[29] Government requirements set out the process and procedures.[30]

In summary, the acquiring party files an application to a minister, stating the purpose of the CPO, its justification, the compensation associated with a specific property.[31] If satisfied, the government inspector advises the Secretary of state. However, objectors can challenge the CPO as specified in the guidance above.

Shemi Esquire, The compatibility of compulsory purchase orders with human rights, 2019; Shemi Esquire, Human Rights and Housing Estate Regeneration, 2020.

[28] *Guidance-on-compulsory-purchase-and-the-crichel-down-rules-for-the-disposal-of-surplus-land-.pdf*
[29] *https://www.legislation.gov.uk/1981/67/section/2*
[30] *Most acts containing enabling powers specify that the procedures in the Acquisition of Land Act 1981, apply to orders made under those powers and an acquiring authority must follow those procedures'.[30] Shemi Esquire, The Rich Have Lawyers, The London Takings, 2020.*
Shemi Esquire, The compatibility of compulsory purchase orders with human rights, 2019; Shemi Esquire, Human Rights and Housing Estate Regeneration, 2020.

[31] *-ggidance-on-compulsory-purchase-and-the-crichel-down-rules-for-the-disposal-of-surplus-land; Shemi Esquire, The Rich Have Lawyers, The London Takings, 2020.*
Shemi Esquire, The compatibility of compulsory purchase orders with human rights, 2019; Shemi Esquire, Human Rights and Housing Estate Regeneration, 2020.

Source of CPO Powers

CPOs are commonly invoked under a specific act of parliament,[32] but can also be triggered by *owners.*[33] while *'public bodies with statutory powers,*[34] *have particular internal guidance .'*[35] For Estate regeneration, local authorities,[36] can use section 226 of the Town and Country Planning Act 1990, to acquire land compulsorily for development and housing purposes,[37] with some restrictions *under section 226(1A).*[38] Similarly, orders will be subject to consideration on their merit if there is *'a compelling case in the public interest.'*[39]

Statutory compensation

Part of the CPO process requires statutory compensation[40] associated with the acquisition of the Land Act 1981 and CPQ (Vesting Declarations) 1981.[41]

---

[32] *https://www.gov.uk/government/publications/compulsory-purchase-and-compensation-booklet-1-procedure*
[33] *By serving purchase notices, or a blight notice under section 150 of the section 150 of the Town and Country Planning 1990 Act, only served in the circumstances listed in schedule 13 to that act 8'.*[33]

[34] *such as 'local authorities, statutory undertakers, some executive agencies, the Homes and Communities Agency, health service bodies, Government ministers,*
[35] *https://www.gov.uk/government/publications/compulsory-purchase-and-compensation-booklet-1-procedure*
[36] *https://moderngov.lambeth.gov.uk/documents/CPOCabinetReport Westbury.pdf; Shemi Esquire, The Rich Have Lawyers, The London Takings, 2020.*
Shemi Esquire, The compatibility of compulsory purchase orders with human rights,2019; Shemi Esquire, Human Rights and Housing Estate Regeneration, 2020.

[37] *Section 246(1).*
[38] *that the 'acquiring authority must not exercise the power unless they think that the proposed development, redevelopment or improvement is likely to contribute to achieving the promotion or improvement of the economic, social or environmental well-being of the area for which the acquiring authority has administrative responsibility.'*[38]
[39] *compulsory-purchase-process-and-the-crichel-down-rules-guidance ,https://www.gov.uk/government/publications/; Shemi Esquire, The Rich Have Lawyers, The London Takings, 2020.*
Shemi Esquire, The compatibility of compulsory purchase orders with human rights,2019; Shemi Esquire, Human Rights and Housing Estate Regeneration, 2020.

[40] *Under the Land compensation Act 1961, Compulsory Purchase Act 1965, LCA 1965 and LCA1973*
[41] *Michael Barnes, The Law of compulsory purchase and compensation*

There are amendments in respect of rehousing, compensation, payment of disturbance and home loss[42] under the DCLG guidance.[43]

Similarly, *Lord Blackburn,*[44] laid down a compensation principle, that stipulates that *'where acquiring authorities arrange to acquire land by agreement, they will pay compensation as if it had not been compulsorily purchased.*[45] It puts the claimant, in the same position they would have been in, in money terms, *but for* the CPO.[46] However, for residents, the prime issue[47] in relation to compensation, is whether the statutory compensation is equitable, just and fair, given that the loss suffered by residents, is more than just mere loss of a physical structure and financial equity.[48]

Justification of CPOs

CPO processes require legal justification for interfering with one's home or property rights, a nexus between the *exercise of CPO powers*[49] and *a public benefit.*[50]

---

[42] *Such as LCA 1973, Localism Act 2011, inter alia*

[43] *ompulsory_purchase_process_and_the_Crichel_Down_Rules_-_guidance_updated, https://assets.publishing.service.gov.uk; Shemi Esquire, The Rich Have Lawyers, The London Takings, 2020.*
Shemi Esquire, The compatibility of compulsory purchase orders with human rights, 2019; Shemi Esquire, Human Rights and Housing Estate Regeneration, 2020.

[44] *Livingstone V Rayward Railway company (1880)*

[45] *DCLG guidance cited above.*

[46] *Denyer-Green, B. (2014). Compulsory Purchase and Compensation. London: Estates Gazette.*

[47] *See A1P1 and compensation below.*

[48] *Shemi Esquire, The Rich Have Lawyers, The London Takings, 2020.*
Shemi Esquire, The compatibility of compulsory purchase orders with human rights, 2019; Shemi Esquire, Human Rights and Housing Estate Regeneration, 2020.

[49] *For estate regeneration,[49] legal justification, should demonstrate, inter alia, a compelling case in the public interest, compatibility with ECHR, consideration of a public sector equality duty, funding sources, viability tests, alternatives to CPO, planning considerations and negotiations with the landowners.*

[50] *See Lord denning in Prest v SOS for wales 1982 who cited Forbes in Brown V SOS for the environment ;Mentions R v SOS transport exparte p de Rothschild, pg. 16; SAINSBURY'S SUPERMARKETS LTD, REGINA (ON THE APPLICATION OF) V WOLVERHAMPTON CITY COUNCIL AND ANOTHER: SC 12 MAY 2010; December 20, 2018 admin Off Planning, Sainsbury Wolverhampton References: [2010] UKSC 20, [2010] RVR 237, [2010] 20 EG 144, [2010] PTSR 1103, [2010] 2 WLR 1173; Shemi Esquire, The Rich Have Lawyers, The London Takings, 2020;*
Shemi Esquire, The compatibility of compulsory purchase orders with human rights, 2019; Shemi Esquire, Human Rights and Housing Estate Regeneration, 2020.

Shemi Esquire

The CPO guidance[51] also necessitates justification for human rights interference. The guidance stipulates that, *'when making and confirming an order, acquiring authorities and authorising authorities should be sure that the purposes for which the compulsory purchase order is made, justify interfering with the human rights of those with an interest in the land affected. Particular consideration should be given to the provisions of Article 1 of the First Protocol to the European Convention on Human Rights and, in the case of a dwelling, Article 8 of the Convention'.*[52]

However, human rights issues risk routinely being interpreted as mere considerations, as opposed to mandatory enforceable legal obligations Consequently, CPOs are challenged, inter alia, for inadequate compensation[53] and *lack of adherence*[54] *to statutory provisions, incompatibility with human rights, lack of satisfaction of the public interest and proportionality,* as discussed below.

Public interest

Satisfying the public interest compelling case criteria is one of the prerequisites for a CPO confirmation.[55] Under the government guidance, there is a requirement for *'a balanced view between the intentions of the acquiring authority, the concerns of those*

---

[51] *Guidance-on-compulsory-purchase-and-the-crichel-down-rules-for-the-disposal-of-surplus-land-pdf.*
[52] *Guidance-on-compulsory-purchase-and-the-crichel-down-rules-for-the-disposal-of-surplus-land-pdf.*
[53] *Estate-regeneration-why-people-power-is-forcing-london-to-rethink-,ttps://www.architectsjournal.co.uk, ;*
The-doomsday-book housing, https://architectsforsocialhousing.wordpress.com/, 2016/03/24/; Phil Hubbard, Loretta Lees. (2018) The right to community? City 22:1, pages 8-25.; https://www.transparency.org.uk/faulty-towers; Paul Watt (2009) Housing Stock Transfers, Regeneration and State-Led Gentrification in London, Urban Policy and Research, 27:3, 229-242, DOI: 10.1080/08111140903154147 5. article
[54] *Bokrosova V Lambeth; http://www.bailii.org/ew/cases/EWHC/Admin/2015/3386.html*
[55] *In Grafton Group (UK) v Sec of state*

with an interest in the land and the wider public interest'.[56] As Laws J states,[57]*'it is enough that ownership in land is recognised as a constitutional right, as Lord Denning said it was. Only another interest, a public interest, of greater interest, may override it followed by a requirement to pay full and fair compensation.'*

Furthermore, under the CPO guidance indicated above presumably drafted with the ECHR jurisprudence in mind, the intrusion must be *'proportionate to the stated aim,'* by applying what is termed as a *'fair balance test.'* The test assesses the justifiable legitimate aim, a rational connection to the aim, use of less intrusive means and consideration of the benefits, juxtaposed to the dis-benefits. Therefore, it is evident , that in determining further association with the public interest, the public sector duty, is an integral component of the CPO approval process, as discussed in detail below.

Public Sector Equality Duty[58]

The CPO guidance emphasises that, *"all public sector acquiring authorities are bound by the Public Sector Equality Duty as set out in section 149 of the Equality Act 2010'.* Notably, it asserts that *'in exercising their compulsory purchase and related powers, acquiring authorities must have regard to the effect of any differential impacts on groups with protected characteristics.'*

---

[56] *cpo_guidance.pdf,https://assets.publishing.service.gov.uk/government/uploads/system/uploads/attachmen271/cpo_guidance.pdf*
[57] *Chesterfield Properties Place v Sec of State (1997) 76 P & CR 117.*
[58] *Public sector duty, under s149 of EA2010*

Shemi Esquire

In the context of estate regeneration, in practice practical implementation is often inadequate,[59] since the process appears self-serving because the acquiring body drives the impact assessments. Hence, for many residents, the process and outcome are not always fair, just, and equitable.[60]

To cure this,[61] the legal fulcrum should focus on the rights of residents, as a mandatory or paramount legal requirement, to guarantee that residents in situ are not displaced from the community, through emphasis a suggested *'right to community.'* The right to community is raised by among others, *Hubbard et al*, who argue, that the focus of the law ought to be on the rights of residents, to stay in their community, could be indicative of an extended conception of housing rights, that culminate into a prospective arguable *'right to community,'* rather than the *'politics of gentrification.'*[62]

In practical legal terms, this could be realised through a robust legal incorporation application and of social, economic and cultural rights, in the CPO process, as an integral framework for the right to community.[63] It would behove the courts to actively

---

[59] *Actual-equalities-study-at-last, https://justspace.org.uk/*
[60] *Shemi Esquire, The Rich Have Lawyers, The London Takings, 2020.*
Shemi Esquire, The compatibility of compulsory purchase orders with human rights, 2019; Shemi Esquire, Human Rights and Housing Estate Regeneration, 2020.

[61] *Hodkinson, Stuart, and Chris Essen. "Grounding accumulation by dispossession in everyday life: The unjust geographies of urban regeneration under the private finance initiative." International Journal of Law in the Built Environment (2015).*
[62]

Hubbard, Phil, and Loretta Lees. "The right to community? Legal geographies of resistance on London's gentrification frontiers." City 22.1 (2018): 8-25.

[63]

Hearne, Rory. "Realising the "right to the city": Developing a human rights-based framework for regeneration of areas of urban disadvantage." International Journal of Law in the Built Environment (2013).

treat human rights in the context of CPOs, as an existential fundamental legal right that needs to be legally and practically enforced, as opposed to a mere consideration.[64]

It should be noted that despite the guidance,[65] the current requirements, could be potentially manipulated, to the detriment of the less resourced and weaker communities. [66] Therefore, aligning the expropriation of homes with the right to community, through emphasis on cultural, social and economic rights, with the human rights requirements of residents, at the centre, would be a more just and effective human rights compliance approach.[67]

Although the existing human rights associated with property, could be utilised to protect residents to a degree, their practical application is debatable, as discussed below.[68]

ECHR Rights

As briefly highlighted above, among other legal requirements, human rights[69] are a fundamental consideration during the CPO authorisation of estate regeneration, by

[64] Shemi Esquire, The Rich Have Lawyers, The London Takings, 2020.
Shemi Esquire, The compatibility of compulsory purchase orders with human rights,2019; Shemi Esquire, Human Rights and Housing Estate Regeneration, 2020.

[65] stipulates that 'the purposes for which the compulsory purchase order is made,' should 'justify interfering with the human rights of those with an interest in the land affected.,
[66] Wightman, Andy. The poor had no lawyers: who owns Scotland and how they got it. Birlinn, 2013.
[67] Hearne, Rory. "Realising the "right to the city": Developing a human rights-based framework for regeneration of areas of urban disadvantage." International Journal of Law in the Built Environment (2013).
[68] Shemi Esquire, The Rich Have Lawyers, The London Takings, 2020.
Shemi Esquire, The compatibility of compulsory purchase orders with human rights,2019; Shemi Esquire, Human Rights and Housing Estate Regeneration, 2020.

[69] See "Tesco Stores Limited v Secretary of State for the Environment and Others (Full Report)". Journal of planning and environment law (0307-4870), p. 581.; Shemi Esquire, The Rich Have Lawyers, The London Takings, 2020.

public authorities. The legal obligations emphasise that *'the purposes for which the compulsory purchase order is made"* should *'justify interfering with the human rights of those with an interest in the land affected.*[70] It is a key ingredient within the ECHR jurisdiction.

Jurisdiction

The United Kingdom is a party to the ECHR[71] which incorporated the Human Rights Act(1998) into UK national law. The Act must be understood and granted effect in compatibility with convention rights, by public authorities, through their processes, decisions or impact thereof. Therefore, public authorities must act in conformity with the ECHR or as commonly put, such authorities should be subjected to the legal jurisdiction of ECtHR[72] and s3 of the HRA 1998.[73]

Section 4 of the HRA 1998 refers to declaration of compatibility of the law but does not necessarily curtail the law. While section 6 renders it *unlawful* for a *public authority to infringe* the ECHR. This may apply to organisations which perform public functions.[74]

Although UK courts do not have a requirement to make identical decisions to the ECHR, the courts ought to consider ECtHR decisions.[75] Any person affected can bring

---

Shemi Esquire, The compatibility of compulsory purchase orders with human rights,2019; Shemi Esquire, Human Rights and Housing Estate Regeneration, 2020.

Publishing.service.gov.uk), DLHC,Guidance-on-compulsory-purchase-and-the-crichel-down-rules-for-the-disposal-of-surplus-land-pdf,2019f

[71] *The Law of compulsory purchase, third edition, Guy Roots et al*
[72] *https://www.legislation.gov.uk/ukpga/1998/section/2*
[73] *See nutshells, Human rights ;(state year?) See also HA1985-s7-Compulsory purchase/Human rights act guide to practitioners-Christopher Baker.*
[74] *https://www.legislation.gov.uk/ukpga/1998/42/section/4*
[75] *https://www.legislation.gov.uk/ukpga/1998/42/section/4*

a legal complaint, but victims need to have standing under the CPO and the court can look at substance rather than form.

A pressure group can be a victim if it shows that it is affected but it is for public authorities to show compatibility with ECHR rights although the complaint faces rejection if it is raised too late.[76]

However, individual states possess what is termed as a *margin of appreciation* in implementation, because housing is considered as part of the social economic policy of a state, which it is argued, may require unique resolutions, unless there is a *manifest unreasonable foundation.*[77] It must be however stressed that, this may be understood from an opposite standpoint of international convention rights, as highlighted by the UN Rapporteur on human rights.[78]

ECHR

The rights protected by the ECHR are sixteen in total which are classified into absolute, limited or qualified categories.[79] Property rights fall in the qualified category but are human rights that are no lesser than any other human rights.[80]

The most applicable human rights articles associated with CPOs to be discussed here include, *Art 8, A1P1, Art 6, of the ECHR* incorporating the HRA 1998, and international

---

[76] *https://www.legislation.gov.uk/ukpga/1998/42/contents*
[77] *ECHR; https://www.echr.coe.int/Convention_ENG.pdf*
[78] *Special Rapporteur on extreme poverty and human rights; https://www.ohchr.orgExtremePoverty*
[79] *Andrew Drzemczewski.*
[80] *https://www.echr.coe.int*

conventions.[81] The reference to international conventions is referred to in A1P1, which specifically refers to principles of law and international law, that underline the payment of compensation, in as far as money can be compensation for the loss of a home, with the associated fundamental life connections, as opposed to a physical structure per se.[82] However, the focus here is on ECHR, starting with art 8 below.

Article 8 and CPOs

Article 8 of ECHR,[83] states that:

1. 'Everyone has the right to respect for his private and family life, his home and his correspondence.

2. There shall be no interference by a public authority with the exercise of this right except such as is in accordance with the law and is necessary in a democratic society in the interests of national security, public safety or the economic well-being of the country, for the prevention of disorder or crime, for the protection of health or morals, or for the protection of the rights and freedoms of others'.[84]

Before discussing in detail, the relevance of art 8, to CPOs under estate regeneration, it is important to explore the jurisdiction, scope and key tenets of art 8.

; *Shemi Esquire, The Rich Have Lawyers, The London Takings, 2020.*
Shemi Esquire, The compatibility of compulsory purchase orders with human rights, 2019; Shemi Esquire, Human Rights and Housing Estate Regeneration, 2020.

[81] *ECHR, https://www.echr.coe.int/*
[82] *https://www.echr.coe.int/*
[83] *Guide_Art_8_ENG.pdf , https://www.echr.coe.int/*
[84] *Guide_Art_8_ENG.pdf , https://www.echr.coe.int/*

Shemi Esquire

Art 8Jurisdiction

Public authorities,[85] such as social housing providers, attract the jurisdiction of HRA 1998 and Art 8 of HRA.[86] And as such, it is strongly arguable that residents affected by CPOs, could utilise Art 8(1), to legally challenge the use of CPOs in the expropriation of their homes, since art 8 clearly reiterates that the *'exercise of the CPO must be in accordance with the law'.*[87]

The potential challenges under art 8 are heightened by the fact that planning and public authorities, possess opaque discretionary powers,[88] which are susceptible to arbitrary use.[89] Such arbitrary use, raises potential incompatibility with Art 8, if applied unlawfully, where there are illegitimate aims or disproportionate actions.[90] In the case of estate regeneration, this affects decisions associated with CPOs, demolition of homes, compensation, valuations and rehousing.

In one such instance, in the case of *Malone*, where the issue involved determination of infringement of rights by surveillance, the court held that although this was consistent with domestic law, discretionary use and application by officers, was arbitrary and therefore incompatible with the ECHR.[91] Apart from the jurisdiction of

---

[85] *Connors V UK (2005) 40 EHRR 9 'gypsies' removal from a locality was violation of art8.*

[86] *R (weaver v London & Quadrant Housing Trust (2009) EWCA Civ 587*

[87] *Malone v UK (1984) ECHR 10*

[88] *Greg Brown & Sean Yeong Wei Chin (2013) Assessing the Effectiveness of Public Participation in Neighbourhood Planning, Planning Practice & Research, 28:5, 563-588, DOI: 10.1080/02697459.2013.820037*

[89] *Too-poor-to-play-children-in-social-housing-blocked-from-communal-playground, https://www.theguardian.com/cities/2019/mar/25/*

[90] *Lustig-Prean and Beckett v UK (1999) ECHR 71 relating to UK military ban on LBGT due to 'operational' issues.*

[91] *Malone v UK (1984) ECHR 10*

art 8, it is important to explain the scope and reach of art 8 and how that may affect CPOs in estate regeneration.[92]

Scope of Art 8

Art 8[93] protects respect for a home as well as deprivation of a home either by way of access or occupation. It safeguards the right to live without interference and intrusion in one's family or private life, correspondence, as well as personal information being kept private and confidential. It requires a positive step from a public authority.

Definition of a home

Home as a general definition is a settled place where one lives, including a home one has the intention to move to,[94] and is described as an autonomous concept not based on domestic law categorisations.[95] To engage Art 8 protection, there must be a determination on facts relating to continuous links and rights, which cannot be interfered with, unless there is a reasonable justification.[96]

There is no general right to housing under HRA or ECHR,[97] except the right of a respect for a home and protection against legally unjustifiable interference of the

---

[92] *Shemi Esquire, The Rich Have Lawyers, The London Takings, 2020.*
Shemi Esquire, The compatibility of compulsory purchase orders with human rights, 2019; Shemi Esquire, Human Rights and Housing Estate Regeneration, 2020.

[93] *ECHR*
[94] *Gillow v UK91986) ECHR 14*
Donoghue V Poplar Housing association (2001) EWACA Civ 595
[95] *, Guide_Art_8_ENG.pdf ,https://www.echr.coe.int/Documents/*
[96]*Guide_Art_8_ENG.pdf, https://www.echr.coe.int/Documents/*
[97] *https://www.echr.coe.int/Documents/Guide_Art_8_ENG.pdf*

peaceful and quiet enjoyment of one's home or possessions. Furthermore, the state has a positive obligation to be proactive in regulating non state interference and to provide remedies against harassment of individuals in and around their home.[98]

Classification of a home under art 8

The ECHR[99] classifies a home as meriting protection under the respect for a home legal principle, extending to property where the complainant is not an owner, tenant, long term occupancy, a relative's house or a care facility.[100]This may not apply to a home that one intends to build.[101]

Although Art 8[102] puts emphasis on a home being non-transient or exceedingly short term, like a hotel room, in the notion of a home was not restricted to being lawfully established.[103]

This could arguably widen the consideration of what a home entails, depending on the specific circumstances of the affected party. But it is doubtful that this would arise in a CPO related scenario, since the physical demarcations are established by both the planning and acquiring authorities, whose interest is in the physical land for demolition purposes, rather than eviction for occupation. It may conceivably be relevant when assessing compensation to the occupant.[104]

---

[98] *Marckx x Belgium (1979) ECHR 2*
[99] *Convention_ENG.pdf , https://www.echr.coe.int/Documents/*
[100] *Convention_ENG.pdf , https://www.echr.coe.int/Documents/*
[101] *Louizdou V Turkey (1996) ECHR 70*
[102] *h Convention_ENG.pdf , ttps://www.echr.coe.int/*
[103] *Buckley v UK,*
[104] *Shemi Esquire, The Rich Have Lawyers, The London Takings, 2020.*

Shemi Esquire

Wider Specific Art 8 protections

Among other rights, Art 8 safeguards rights such as succession, contracts of parties and the protection of a positive duty to child integration, since family law matters relate to a family home.[105] This is not applicable to fiancées but extends to benefits or allowances indicating the respect for their family life.[106] This is relevant to residents facing CPOs, who are not physically in occupation but may impact their re-housing, compensation and succession rights. Equally, there may be preconditions imposed on residents,[107] whose occupation rights had ceased as well as short-term occupants after the displacement of secure tenants[108] during the so-called *decanting CPO* process.[109]

The added significance is that, due to the cost of housing, which is exacerbated by welfare cuts, sub renting or sharing homes is an affordable way to live[110] or work in some cities.[111] Although, there may not be agreements with the landlords, there is a

---

Shemi Esquire, The compatibility of compulsory purchase orders with human rights,2019; Shemi Esquire, Human Rights and Housing Estate Regeneration, 2020.

[105] *Guide_Art_8_ENG.pdf ,https://www.echr.coe.int/*
[106] *Guide_Art_8_ENG.pdf ,https://www.echr.coe.int/*
[107] *http://estateregeneration.lambeth.gov.uk/key_guarantees#homeowners; Shemi Esquire, The Rich Have Lawyers, The London Takings, 2020.*
Shemi Esquire, The compatibility of compulsory purchase orders with human rights,2019; Shemi Esquire, Human Rights and Housing Estate Regeneration, 2020.

[108] *Part IV of HA 1985 amended by HA1988 and HA 96.*
[109] *Alice Belotti LSE Housing & Communities, Estate Regeneration and Community Impacts Challenges and lessons for social landlords, developers and local councils, Case report 99, March 2016; Shemi Esquire, The Rich Have Lawyers, The London Takings, 2020.*
Shemi Esquire, The compatibility of compulsory purchase orders with human rights,2019; Shemi Esquire, Human Rights and Housing Estate Regeneration, 2020.

[110] *Fenton, Alex. "Housing benefit reform and the spatial segregation of low-income households in London." (2011).*
[111] *Hamnett, Chris. "Moving the poor out of central London? The implications of the coalition government 2010 cuts to Housing Benefits." Environment and Planning A 42.12 (2010): 2809-2819.*

need for a level of legal protection beyond the narrow confines of statutory or contractual arrangements.[112] Especially, in circumstances where occupants do not fit the traditional version of a home, as highlighted in *Chapman V UK,*[113] where the concept of a home was expanded to cabins and bungalows stationed on land, as well as second homes, irrespective of legality under national law.[114]

However, sufficient nexus or occupation is necessary for recognition of a right to a home. There are limitations if there is minimal occupation, weak links to the property or if connections were expunged. Likewise, a mere possibility of inheritance may not give rise to a connection to a home under Art 8.[115] However, altering the terms of tenancy[116] was found to be interference in Art 8.[117]

On that basis, it is certainly arguable, that the demolition of one's home, through compulsory confiscation,[118] which involves cancellation of contracts, mortgages and physical occupation, attracts protection under Art 8.[119] Particularly when there is compulsion to move from the home, land and locality in some instances. A clear interference in the respect to a home and therefore triggering potential art 8 challenge.[120]

---

[112] Michael Edwards (2016) The housing crisis and London, City, 20:2, 222-237, DOI: 10.1080/13604813.2016.1145947
[113] Chapman-v-united-kingdom-application-no-2723895
[114] https://www.echr.coe.int/Guide_Art_8_ENG.pdf
[115] https://www.echr.coe.int/Guide_Art_8_ENG.pdf
[116] Loretta Lees, The Urban Injustices of New Labour's "New Urban Renewal": The Case of the Aylesbury Estate in London, 2013
[117] (Berger-Krall and Others v. Slovenia, § 264).
[118] (Aboufadda v. France (Dec.)).
[119] Selçuk and Asker v. Turkey, § 86; Akdivar and Others v. Turkey [GC], § 88; Menteş and Others v. Turkey, § 73).
[120] Noack and Others v. Germany (Dec.)).

Shemi Esquire

Apart from the above issues, residents facing CPOs are often faced with multiple challenges regarding their homes and wider communities. Among those is the resulting disrepair, blight and anti-social behaviour, as briefly highlighted below.

Disrepair or blight

As stated above, in areas where CPO processes are triggered, disrepair or neglect is a common feature.[121] Disrepair[122] has been found to be an infringement of Art 8,[123] after an examination of procedural guarantees to determine the margin of appreciation. This is relevant to CPO[124] affected residents, who face a process which is characterised with a lack of transparency, imbalance of resources and conflicts of interest associated with local authorities.[125]

Disrepair and the consequential social ills associated with estate demolitions, are legally the responsibilities of the local authorities to prevent, remedy and prosecute. Yet, CPO planning decisions by local authorities,[126] are also authorised by the same

---

[121] *Estate Regeneration and Community Impacts Challenges and lessons for social landlords, developers and local councils, Case report 99, Alice Belotti LSE Housing & Communities March 2016.*
See also Save Cressingham gardens; Save Central Hill: @savewetburysw8
[122] *(Khamidov v. Russia,*
[123] *Novoseletskiy v. Ukraine, §§ 84-88).*
[124] *Estate Regeneration and Community Impacts Challenges and lessons for social landlords, developers and local councils, Case report 99, Alice Belotti LSE Housing & Communities March 2016; See also Save Cressingham gardens.; Shemi Esquire, The Rich Have Lawyers, The London Takings, 2020.*
Shemi Esquire, The compatibility of compulsory purchase orders with human rights,2019; Shemi Esquire, Human Rights and Housing Estate Regeneration, 2020.

[125] *See inter alia Hackworth & Smith, 2001; Glynn, 2008; Lees et al., 2008; Shaw, 2008, argue that Stock transfer in London can be understood through the lens of state-led 'third-wave gentrification', a widespread phenomenon across British, North American and Australian cities. ; Shemi Esquire, The Rich Have Lawyers, The London Takings, 2020.*
Shemi Esquire, The compatibility of compulsory purchase orders with human rights,2019; Shemi Esquire, Human Rights and Housing Estate Regeneration, 2020.

[126] *Buckley v. the United Kingdom, § 60).*

acquiring party, which would appear to be a prima facie conflict of interest to the detriment of impacted residents.[127]

On the theme of potential self-interest, the *Kate Barker Report,* regarding the use of land for planning,[128] refers to *'planning decisions as policy decisions or expediency decisions* conducted in *'an anomalous manner subject to a degree of judicial review.'*[129]

This could be regarded as a feasible indication that there is an absence of independent processes in planning matters, which can be characterised as an intrusion with the 'respect for a home,' under art 8, in terms of independence and impartiality, under art 6.

It must be noted that such interference can be qualified under A1P1, which[130] affords a member state, to maintain a *'degree of traditional, national or domestic approach'*,[131] and criteria.[132] However, if the right in point is crucial to the person's human rights, the courts minimise the margin of appreciation.[133] This was evidenced in *Connors v the United Kingdom*, where the court stated that, *'the loss of one's home, is a most extreme form of interference with the right to respect for the home'.* The case

---

[127] Siobhan O'Sullivan, et al. "Hearing the Voices of Children and Youth in Housing Estate Regeneration." Children, Youth and Environments, vol. 27, no. 3, 2017, pp. 1–15. JSTOR, www.jstor.org/27.3.0001.
[128] J.P.L 1570
[129] Shemi Esquire, The Rich Have Lawyers, The London Takings, 2020.
Shemi Esquire, The compatibility of compulsory purchase orders with human rights, 2019; Shemi Esquire, Human Rights and Housing Estate Regeneration, 2020.

[130] (Howard v. the United Kingdom,
[131] Alec Samuels, The planning process and judicial control: the case for better judicial involvement and control, J.P.L 1570
[132] Noack and Others v. Germany (dec.))
[133] (Connors v. the United Kingdom, § 82).

concerned an *'eviction from a caravan site'* on the basis that the occupant had no licence. The court found that art 8 was breached due to the absence of a justification for such interference as well as the absence of a *pressing social need* to warrant the eviction.[134]

Art 8 and Private life

Private life is interpreted widely to include *'personal and physical integrity.'*[135]The relevancy to CPOs is the excessive unjustifiable intrusion into people's lives culminating to eventual displacement. This extends to collection of personal data,[136]especially for vulnerable residents [137], lack of full provision of information,[138] due to a lack of access to independent advice. The process allows the public authorities, usually also the acquiring authority, in the case of estate regeneration, to arguably gain competitive negotiation, commercial and legal advantage over residents, through characteristically compelled disclosure of personal information. Such intrusive compelled disclosure requires justification to avoid contravention of Art 8,[139] since art 8 protection extends to providing information for census purposes including surveys.[140]

---

[134] *CONNORS v. THE UNITED KINGDOM - 66746/01 [2004] ECHR 223 (27 May 2004) (bailii.org); Shemi Esquire, The Rich*

[135] *X and Y v the Netherlands (1985) ECHR 4*

[136] *Jane Rendell (2017) 'Arry's Bar: condensing and displacing on the Aylesbury Estate, The Journal of Architecture, 22:3, 532-554, DOI: 10.1080/13602365.2017.1310125*

[137] *http://newmanfrancis.org/projects/westbury-lambeth/*

[138] *https://www.ucl.ac.uk/engineering-exchange/sites/engineering-exchange/files/fact-sheet-health-and-wellbeing-social-housing.pdf*

[139] *As held in, Hilton V UK Application no,12015/86*

[140] *Z v Finland (1997) 25 EHHR 371*

Additionally, Intrusion in private life further includes loss of support networks in the locality, the disruption to professional associations,[141] loss of employment[142] as well as the impact it has on *'relationships, material well-being, family and reputation', in the perspective of art 8 under ECHR.*[143]

Besides, the intrusion or interference into one's intimate and family life, another key aspect, is the fairness, independence and impartiality of the CPO process and how that intersects with art 8.[144] An issue that is discussed below but in greater detail under art 6, separately.

Fair process

Estate regeneration decisions and processes may not be meaningfully understood or formal, during a disruptive protracted process for residents. Yet valuations, advance payments, negotiations for compensation or rehousing, typically require specialist technical advice or access to financial resources.[145]

---

[141] *Volkov Ukraine (21722/11) 2013 IRLR 480(ECtHR),*

[142] *Practical Law UK practice Note 8 835 5732.*

[143] *Shemi Esquire, The Rich Have Lawyers, The London Takings, 2020.*
Shemi Esquire, The compatibility of compulsory purchase orders with human rights, 2019; Shemi Esquire, Human Rights and Housing Estate Regeneration, 2020.

[144] *Shemi Esquire, The Rich Have Lawyers, The London Takings, 2020.*
Shemi Esquire, The compatibility of compulsory purchase orders with human rights, 2019; Shemi Esquire, Human Rights and Housing Estate Regeneration, 2020.

[145] *Stuart Hodkinson, Chris Essen, (2015) "Grounding accumulation by dispossession in everyday life: The unjust geographies of urban regeneration under the Private Finance Initiative", International Journal of Law in the Built Environment, Vol. 7 Issue: 1, pp.72-91, https://doi.org/10.1108/IJLBE-01-2014-0007*

Characteristically, valuations are determined largely by the either the acquiring authority or organisations appointed by them, with limited independent oversight over the imposition of pre-conditions and where there are valuation disputes.[146] The threat of intrusion on this scale, should in principle have the *proportionality* of the measure scrutinised by an impartial court, under the framework Article 8.[147]

It is strongly arguable, that CPO key processes, at a considerably basic level, should be conducted, in a *'manner that respects the human dignity of affected persons and give respect to their home,*[148] *giving appropriate weight to individual circumstances.'*[149] An issue that was highlighted in *Connors,*[150]where *it was held that the* 'gypsies 'removal from a locality was violation of Art 8. The authority in question evaded statutory requirements, when it made the claimant's spouse *'sign a notice to quit,'* without due regard to *'respect for his home.'* Therefore, this accentuates the need for transparency, by public authorities, where compulsory loss of a home is the outcome. A failure to do that can cumulatively lead to evictions, discussed in detail below.

Evictions

---

[146] *Estate Regeneration and Community Impacts Challenges and lessons for social landlords, developers and local councils, Case report 99, Alice Belotti LSE Housing & Communities March 2016; See also Save Cressingham gardens.*
See inter alia Hackworth & Smith, 2001; Glynn, 2008; Lees et al., 2008; Shaw, 2008, argue that Stock transfer in London can be understood through the lens of state-led 'third-wave gentrification', a widespread phenomenon across British, North American and Australian cities.; Shemi Esquire, The Rich Have Lawyers, The London Takings, 2020.
Shemi Esquire, The compatibility of compulsory purchase orders with human rights, 2019; Shemi Esquire, Human Rights and Housing Estate Regeneration, 2020.

[147] *(McCann v. the United Kingdom, § 50)*
[148] *(Rousk v. Sweden, §§ 137-142).*
[149] *(Gillow v. the United Kingdom, §§ 56-58).*
[150] *Connors V UK (2005) 40 EHRR*

As briefly mentioned, during the CPO process, there are various arbitrary measures, which could lead to evictions. Such measures include planning processes, inept consultation, unilateral changes of tenancies by public authorities, compulsory purchase of leaseholder's homes, unfair valuation processes and inequitable compensation.[151]

Added to that is the physical, as well as the psychological impact of construction elements, such as noise, dust and hazardous construction elements. A combination that results into anti-social behaviours triggered by the decimation of communities due housing estate regeneration.[152]

The cumulative effect of these coercive measures, is that residents are compelled to move from their homes under duress, in ostensibly weaker bargaining positions than the local authorities who are also the acquiring authorities.[153] In effect, residents are compelled to move or are evicted from their homes and their local community,[154] often under arbitrary and vague measures, without meaningful access to independent legal advice in various instances.[155]

---

[151] Shemi Esquire, The Rich Have Lawyers, The London Takings, 2020.
Shemi Esquire, The compatibility of compulsory purchase orders with human rights, 2019; Shemi Esquire, Human Rights and Housing Estate Regeneration, 2020.

[152] The Southall Stench: Developer facing Legal Action over Remediation, todaysconveyancer.co.uk;

Substances released at Southall site are 'threat to health' - BBC News

[153] Hodkinson, Stuart. "Not fit for purpose: The Myatts Field North PFI horror show." Safe as houses. Manchester University Press, 2020. 121-158 ; Hodkinson, Stuart, and Chris Essen. "Grounding accumulation by dispossession in everyday life: The unjust geographies of urban regeneration under the private finance initiative." International Journal of Law in the Built Environment (2015).
[154] Jane Rendell (2017) 'Arry's Bar: condensing and displacing on the Aylesbury Estate, The Journal of Architecture, 22:3, 532-554, DOI: 10.1080/13602365.2017.1310125;

[155] Duty to give reasons: https://www.lawgazette.co.uk/legal-updates/local-government-duty-to-give-reasons.

The evictions are worsened by local authorities' strained adherence to the duty to give reasons, as required by a public authority. It is an established principle that a public officer making a decision, has a legal obligation to provide explanations for the decisions reached. Simply because providing reasons for decisions, is a significant aspect in securing one's rights in any democratic and rule of law-based society.[156] Especially where *'the decision-maker is disagreeing with a considered and reasoned recommendation.'*[157]

Clearly residents face formidable hurdles to overcome CPO associated measures that could result in evictions. Despite the hurdles, arbitrary measures could be challenged by the affected parties, in principle, under art 8, in intersection with art 6. However, it must be emphasised that the realistic remedial application and the positive effect of art 8, in evictions, has wavered over the course of time, as briefly examined below.[158]

Evolving evictions case law and ECHR

---

[156] *A. P. Le Sueur, Legal Duties to Give Reasons, Current Legal Problems, Volume 52, Issue 1, 1999, Pages 150–172, https://doi.org/10.1093/clp/52.1.150*
[157] *Local government, duty to give reasons, https://www.lawgazette.co.uk; Shemi Esquire, The Rich Have Lawyers, The London Takings, 2020.*
Shemi Esquire, The compatibility of compulsory purchase orders with human rights, 2019; Shemi Esquire, Human Rights and Housing Estate Regeneration, 2020.

[158] *Donoghue, above; CONNORS v. THE UNITED KINGDOM - 66746/01 [2004] ECHR 223 (27 May 2004) (bailii.org); Shemi Esquire, The Rich Have Lawyers, The London Takings, 2020.*
Shemi Esquire, The compatibility of compulsory purchase orders with human rights, 2019; Shemi Esquire, Human Rights and Housing Estate Regeneration, 2020

Analysis Of The Human Rights Impact Of Estate Regeneration In the United Kingdom

Shemi Esquire

Over time, the courts appear to have recognised, a legitimate deployment of art 8 in eviction proceedings, raising the proportionality of such measures, as highlighted in *Pinnock*.[159] However, notwithstanding the elements in *Pinnock,* the court still held that the eviction could still proceed, despite, the court's agreement, which indicated that there should have been a mechanism where Mr Pinnock, had *'an opportunity of having the proportionality of the measure determined by a court, and having any relevant issue of fact resolved'.* Therefore, the potential success in *Pinnock* seems to be a narrow legal remit which arguably provides modest relief to residents faced with evictions under CPOs. It also remains a cumbersome process for residents, in the absence of expeditious avenues to pertinent legal advice and economic resources.

However, *Pinnock*, remains a strong development and requires a degree of analysis to determine its practical efficacy in terms of legal relief. The key issues were:

(a) *'whether article 8 of the European Convention on Human Rights ("the Convention") requires a court, which is being asked to make an order for possession under section 143D(2) of the Housing Act 1996 ("the 1996 Act") against a person occupying premises under a demoted tenancy, to have the power to consider whether the order would be "necessary in a democratic society".*

(b) *if so, whether section 143D(2) is compatible with article 8 of the Convention ("article 8"). In the result, the Court answers both questions in the affirmative.'*

Specifically, to the question of the eviction, the court rejected the appeal and maintained the order for possession. Stating that, *'Mr Pinnock is, and was, entitled to an opportunity of having the proportionality of the measure determined by a court, and,*

---

[159] *Manchester City Council v Pinnock [2010] UKSC 45 (03 November 2010) (bailii.org)*

if necessary for that purpose, of having any relevant issue of fact resolved. That right was not acknowledged by the courts below (for wholly understandable reasons). We have, however, afforded him the opportunity to have the proportionality of the possession order considered. Having considered the issue, we are satisfied that it was proportionate to make the order, irrespective of the truth relating to the two possible issues of fact between Mr Pinnock and the Council.'

As specified above, the court still held that the eviction could proceed, despite, the court's agreement, stressing the need for an avenue where Mr Pinnock had *'an opportunity of having the proportionality of the measure determined by a court and having any relevant issue of fact resolved.'*

The probable implication of the courts conclusions appears to be, that the court was satisfied that there was an opportunity to review or determine the measures in question, in this case, an eviction. Juxtaposing this to estate expropriation and supplanting that rationale, residents could still face eviction if local authorities provided opportunities to have measures, processes reviewed or determined by an independent tribunal or process. This could be by way of judicial review or via the CPO process itself, including the secretary of state. However, there are considerable practical, financial and structural impediments that make access to judicial review or the CPO process, a largely academic issue for residents which appears to suit the local authorities with deep pockets with access to specialist advice.

Therefore, under art 8, if this logic were followed, the conclusion of the court in *Pinnock* above, art 8 could only conceivably offer academic rather than practical and meaningful prevention of eviction of estate regeneration affected residents.

Shemi Esquire

In another case, *Connor*[160] the ECtHR, was emphatic in recognising the need for procedural rail guards against arbitrary decisions, by requiring a need to establish a firm justification for interference in the rights. This was aligned with what was characterised by the court as a' *pressing social need' or proportionately* pursuant to the reference by the court as a *'legitimate aim.'* The characterisation further highlights the need to have such measures to be determined by an independent tribunal which is a significant departure from the contract property rights approach in cases such as *Qazi.*[161]

Crucially the principles laid down, in the cases, highlighted above, emphasise that the stated opportunity of a judicial review did not provide sufficient procedural protections for evictions. However, the depth of consideration of the proportionality, remains to be tested in the distance of time. Unfortunately, for impacted residents, at the current rate of estate expropriations, in areas like Lambeth, in London, this may not be sufficient or timely to prevent current evictions associated with CPOs.[162]

Fundamentally, therefore, given the context of the current legal stance on proportionality under art 8, which has yet to stand the test of time, the question that follows is how objectors can have a degree of certainty, as to what the legal and factual circumstances are, where proportionality would be upheld. This would possibly require

---

[160] *CONNORS v. THE UNITED KINGDOM - 66746/01 [2004] ECHR 223 (27 May 2004) (bailii.org)*
[161] *London Borough of Harrow (Appellants) v. Qazi (FC) (Respondent), London Borough of Harrow v. Qazi [2003] UKHL 43 (31 July 2003) (bailii.org)*
[162] *Modern Law Review/2012 - Volume 75/Issue 1, 1 January/Case Notes/"Yeah but, no but' — Pinnock and Powell in the Supreme Court – (2012) 75(1) MLR 78–91*

further cases, in the near future to be determined. However, there are potential implications which are briefly discussed below.

The Implications of the above cases for CPO affected residents

As discussed above, in determining the approval of CPOs, courts examine the lawfulness of the *public good or interest* test and the proportionality of the measure, to the CPO. One of the rationales provided for CPOs, by the acquiring parties, is the need to provide more social homes. However, evidence appears to suggest that there is a loss of social homes at least in some fifty estates. This is exacerbated by the forced displacement caused by the exorbitant costs of the new housing, the prohibitive cost of service charges, the restrictive contracts, utilities and associated bills. Which makes such housing simply unaffordable for many residents who are then forced to leave their homes and communities.[163]

The cumulative aspects of both the loss of social homes and the consequential displacement of residents, with related spiral effects, raises questions as to whether that is consistent with the public interest rationale that is deployed to justify the CPO evictions.

Therefore, as indicated above, in conjunction with the lack of clear practical demonstration of a pattern of a successful proportionality argument, which has stood the test of time, it would appear that art 8, offers aspirational rather than firm protection against evictions via CPOs.

---

[163] *Watt, Paul. "Social housing and urban renewal: An introduction." Social Housing and Urban Renewal. Emerald Publishing Limited, 2017.; Hodkinson, Stuart. "Not fit for purpose: The Myatts Field North PFI horror show." Safe as houses. Manchester University Press, 2020. 121-158.*

In that respect, there is need for a fundamental departure from the *'respect for a home'* standard applied by the courts under art 8, towards a legal principle that gives real protection from arbitrary evictions, especially via CPOs, in the absence of ordinary tenancy related contractual breaches.

With that context, the legal system as it stands, appears to enable and polish the path of CPO evictions, as an agent of dispossession, rather than a fair arbiter against predatory measures that affect the weak and the most marginalised in society. In the case of estate regeneration, the winners seem to be the developers, in concert with local acquiring authorities,[164] which supports the wider argument that the law has historically,[165] in certain aspects, tended to favour the powerful or landowners. And in the case of CPOs, there are clear imbalances of resources and meaningful access independent legal resources, by the evicted residents, which would appear to support that view.[166]

Therefore, art 8 needs to be legally positioned to protect the weak against evictions, by treating the home as a basic guaranteed human need rather than balancing a nuance, regarding notions of proportionality and what amounts to respect for a home. Furthermore, art 8 should ideally provide more clear certainty as to what factual or legal circumstances would warrant the court to uphold such a case under the principle of proportionality.

---

[164] *Hodkinson, Stuart, and Chris Essen. "Grounding accumulation by dispossession in everyday life: The unjust geographies of urban regeneration under the private finance initiative." International Journal of Law in the Built Environment (2015).*
[165] *Nichols, Robert. Theft Is Property! dispossession and critical theory. Duke University Press, 2020. Shemi Esquire, The Rich Have Lawyers, The London Takings, 2020.*
Shemi Esquire, The compatibility of compulsory purchase orders with human rights, 2019; Shemi Esquire, Human Rights and Housing Estate Regeneration, 2020.

[166] *Wightman, Andy. The poor had no lawyers: who owns Scotland and how they got it. Birlinn, 2013.*

Nuisance

Parties who may not possess direct proprietary interest may trigger proportionality, under Art 8. This would be the consideration of the extent to which whether measures taken, were proportional to the abrogation of art 8 key principle of a *respect for a person's home.* Such as the case where a tree was felled into a neighbour's garden.[167] In essence, this view could be extended to construction nuisances, asbestos or contaminants, which is a common feature for estate regeneration residents. Although Art 8 does not offer an inherent protection of a clean environment, per se, such planning decisions interfere with people's homes and family lives, therefore triggering Art 8 and A1P1.[168] An Argument that could be deployed to challenge CPOs in estate regeneration.[169]

Art 8-conclusion

---

[167] *Lane V the Royal Borough of Kensington and Chelsea London Borough Council (2013) EWHC 1320(QB)*
[168] *J.P.L 2010,3 298-309*
[169] *Shemi Esquire, The Rich Have Lawyers, The London Takings, 2020.*
Shemi Esquire, The compatibility of compulsory purchase orders with human rights,2019; Shemi Esquire, Human Rights and Housing Estate Regeneration, 2020.

Analysis Of The Human Rights Impact Of Estate Regeneration In the United Kingdom

Shemi Esquire

As an overview, the ECHR regarded as a *living instrument,*[170] should be construed to align with contemporary circumstances,[171] in order to balance the rights of residents affected by[172] estate regeneration.[173]

Among the effects of estate expropriation, is the impact on longstanding communities,[174] displaced from their localities, their families and support *systems.*[175] The displacement and dislocation abrogates the '*essential ingredient of a family, the right to live together, enjoy each other's' company'* [176] *and relationship development'.*[177] Crucially, the '*notion of family life'* is regarded as an '*autonomous concept',*[178] and therefore appears to largely remain an academic exercise, under art 8, due to the detrimental impact resulting from estate expropriation.[179]

---

[170]

Shachor-Landau, Chava. "The European Convention on Human Rights (ECHR), 1950, as a Living Instrument in the Twenty-First Century." Israel Yearbook on Human Rights, Volume 45 (2015). Brill Nijhoff, 2015. 169-189. ; Letsas, George. "The ECHR as a living instrument: Its meaning and legitimacy." Constituting Europe: The European Court of Human Rights in a National, European and Global Context 2 (2013): 106.; Lawson, R. A. "The ECHR at 70: A Living Instrument in Precarious Present-day Conditions." Leiden Law Blog (2020).

[171] *J.P.L 2010, 3 298-309*
[172] *https://www.echr.coe.int/Documents/Guide_Art_8_ENG.pdf*
[173] *Shemi Esquire, The compatibility of compulsory purchase orders with human rights, 2019.*

Shemi Esquire, Human Rights and Housing Estate Regeneration, 2020; Shemi Esquire, The Rich Have Lawyers: The London Takings , 2020;

[174] *Paul Watt (2013) 'It's not for us', City, 17:1, 99-118, DOI: 10.1080/13604813.2012.754190*
[175] *Tom Slater (2009) Missing Marcuse: On gentrification and displacement, City, 13:2-3, 292-311, DOI: 10.1080/13604810902982250*
[176] *Olson v Sweden*
[177] *Marckx v Belgium*
[178] *Marckx v Belgium; https://www.echr.coe.int /Guide_Art_8_ENG.pdf*
[179] *Shemi Esquire, The Rich Have Lawyers, The London Takings, 2020.*
Shemi Esquire, The compatibility of compulsory purchase orders with human rights, 2019; Shemi Esquire, Human Rights and Housing Estate Regeneration, 2020.

Hence, while there are pronounced protections under art 8, the practical application for CPO affected residents under estate regeneration, appears ambiguous, especially when evictions are the key issue.

Hence, as highlighted above, art 8 needs to be legally positioned to protect the weak against evictions, by treating the home as a basic guaranteed human need or right. As opposed to taking legally nuanced notions of proportionality or as to what amounts to s *respect for a home.*

Furthermore, and perhaps more importantly, art 8, as discussed, should provide more legal certainty and resoluteness, as to what factual or legal circumstances would entail cases to be upheld under the principle of proportionality.

A failure to provide such certainty, creates a vacuum that leads to continued avoidable evictions, to the detriment of residents.

Beyond art 8, as a critical aspect for the *respect for one's home*, as classified under the ECHR, the fairness of the decision-making processes, covered under art 6 of the ECHR, is a fundamental tenet of the rights of residents facing CPOs in estate regeneration.[180]

It is discussed in detail below.

---

[180] *Shemi Esquire, The Rich Have Lawyers, The London Takings, 2020.*
Shemi Esquire, The compatibility of compulsory purchase orders with human rights, 2019; Shemi Esquire, Human Rights and Housing Estate Regeneration, 2020.

Art 6

Art 6 (1) of the ECHR states that, "in the determination of his civil rights and obligations or of any criminal charge against him, everyone is entitled to a fair and public hearing within a reasonable time by an independent and impartial tribunal established by law'.

Art 6(1) is applicable to property rights, privacy matters, internal hearings or processes, in terms of procedural fairness, access to an independent tribunal or equality of arms. Although Art 6 is not absolute,[181] it refers to some procedural limits as acceptable, without procedural guarantees at every stage but stresses access to a court with full jurisdiction.[182]

A key issue is whether a civil right in Art 6 is *'a private right as opposed to a public right'.*[183] Housing is consistent with a civil right, in the context of ECHR and international conventions.[184]

It is the civil arm of Art 6 that is applicable to estate regeneration, requiring an identifiable issue over *rights* that have jurisdiction in domestic law,[185] context, boundaries and application of that right.[186] This is due to competing interests between

---

[181] *Ashingdale v UK (1985) 7 EHRR 528*
[182] *Golder V UK (1975) EHRR 524*
[183] *Alec Samuels, The planning process and judicial control: the case for better judicial involvement and control, J.P.L 1570*
[184] *Kenna, P. (2008). Housing rights: positive duties and enforceable rights at the European Court of Human Rights. European ;*
Shemi Esquire, The Rich Have Lawyers, The London Takings, 2020.
Shemi Esquire, The compatibility of compulsory purchase orders with human rights, 2019; Shemi Esquire, Human Rights and Housing Estate Regeneration, 2020.

Human Rights Law Review, 13(2), 193-208
[185] *H V Belgium (1987) 8 EHH 123 and GEorgiadis V Greece*
[186] *Bentehm V Netherlands (1985 8 EHRR*

parties, such as during consultation, the need for a[187]fair hearing, an expeditious process, access to rehousing[188]and timely compensation. An independent and fair process can be apportioned into procedural or substantive fairness which need a more detailed analysis.

Procedural fairness in the context of CPOs and estate regeneration

Procedural fairness was an issue in *Ali V UK,*[189] where an applicant should have been afforded access to a *'fair hearing before an independent and impartial tribunal.'* In estate regeneration related processes, the decision-making process is characteristically structurally advantageous to and conducted by acquiring authorities. This position favours their legal and commercial interests which is arguably against statutory standards of what would be regarded as meaningful legally compliant *consultation.[190]*

The issue of consultation was one of the key points, in *Bokrosova V Lambeth[191]*, where the court ruled that Lambeth council, had acted unlawfully. The judgment indicated that the process of consultation, *'must include sufficient reasons for the proposals to enable consultees to consider them and respond to them intelligently; enough time must be given for that; and the consultation responses must be taken conscientiously into account when the decision is taken…. ensure public participation in the local*

---

[187] *Bokrosova v LLB http://www.bailii.org/ew/cases/EWHC/Admin/2015/3386.html*
[188] *Begum v London Borough of Tower Hamlets (2003) UKHL 5*
[189] *Ali V UK (2016) 63 HRR 20,*
[190] *Alice Belotti, Estate regeneration and community impact, http://sticerd.lse.ac.uk/dps/case/cr/casereport99.pdf*
[191] *(2015) EWHC 3386(ADMIN)*

authority's decision-making process and ... for consultation to achieve that objective,

it must fulfil basic minimum requirements.'

The judgement in *Bokrosova*, highlights the inbuilt inequality in the entire process. In this case, is based on estate regeneration in Cressingham gardens estate. But its experiences are replicate across the borough of Lambeth repeatedly and would be arguably mirror other estates. In that respect, the systemic nature of such unlawful consultation, in estate regeneration under CPOs, requires a detailed analysis and urgent overhaul.[192]

Access to an impartial tribunal

Pursuing legal action could possibly, theoretically attempt to meet the requirement of access to a fair and impartial hearing or tribunal. However, prohibitive costs bar aggrieved residents from this course of action, especially leaseholders who risk cost orders,[193] in addition to requirements for leave to be sought prior to commencement of legal proceedings.[194]

Parties to estate regeneration processes with deep pockets, such as public bodies or property developers, may also unreasonably delay or deny residents' rights. In other

---

[192] *Douglas, Pam, and Joanne Parkes. "'Regeneration'and 'consultation'at a Lambeth council estate: The case of Cressingham Gardens." City 20.2 (2016): 287-291.; Douglas, Pam, and Joanne Parkes. "'Regeneration'and 'consultation'at a Lambeth council estate: The case of Cressingham Gardens." City 20.2 (2016): 287-291.; Shemi Esquire, The Rich Have Lawyers, The London Takings, 2020.*
Shemi Esquire, The compatibility of compulsory purchase orders with human rights,2019; Shemi Esquire, Human Rights and Housing Estate Regeneration, 2020.

[193] *part-44-general-rules-about-costs, www.justice.gov.uk/courts/procedure-rules/c*
[194] *H V UK, Application no 11559/85*

Shemi Esquire

words, there needs to be active enforcement under art 6 to provide a meaningful opportunity for the full circumstances to be fairly, diligently and impartially determined to prevent abuse of process or punitive penalties.[195]

In that context, estate regeneration affected residents could therefore engage Art 6 if they were subjected to a blanket rule that bars them from bringing civil actions against the acquiring authority. However, attention is drawn to the ruling in *Z and others V UK*[196], that clarified that, *'the inability of applicants to sue the local authority flowed from the principles governing the substantive right of action in negligence as opposed to immunity.'*

National law and Art 6

Engagement of Art 6 requires a disputable implementation of national law, in a specific matter.[197] This was highlighted in *Lithgow,* where the nationalisation of property, under a local Act,[198] was found to engage Art 6 after the applicants alleged lack of statutory compensation. [199] Therefore, where there are unreasonable or disproportionate barriers, deriving from state laws to a person's rights, Art 6 could be engaged. But the issue ought to be of a decisive nature to the rights of an affected party,[200] such as a home, person, family or business affected, hence engaging art 6.

---

[195] *Osman V UK (2000) 29 EHRR 245 (1998) ECHR 101 (1999) 1 LGRT 431*
[196] *Z and others V UK (2001) ECHRR 333, (2002) 34 EHRR 9*
[197] *Lithgow v UK*
[198] *Aircraft and Shipbuilding industries ACT 1977*
[199] *Practical Law Practice note 835 5732.*
[200] *Practical Law Practice note 835 5732.*

Analysis Of The Human Rights Impact Of Estate Regeneration In the United Kingdom

Shemi Esquire

In *Koning V Germany,* [201]a civil right, under ECHR, was of *substantive character* and was defined autonomously, irrespective of characterisation under national law.[202] Similarly, in *Brugger V Austria*, it was held that the complainant was entitled to an oral hearing given that judicial review was not available as remedy in the jurisdiction.[203]

It should be noted that the absence of legal aid is an inherent disadvantage and barrier for disenfranchised residents to challenge decisions. Especially leaseholders who risk substantial cost orders, despite legal aid being necessary in civil proceedings.[204]

Under art 6, issues such as valuation disputes should arguably be determined by an independent tribunal[205] to avoid incompatibility with Art 6.[206] Similarly, under art 6, dispute resolution ought to expeditiously and meaningfully consider individual circumstances, as held in *Robins v UK,* where there was a breach of Art 6[207] due to an unreasonable delay. Since housing expropriation processes tend to be protracted,[208]the practical effect is that acquiring authorities have extensive resources, unlike individual residents, which impacts the negotiation powers. Residents in some cases, are compelled to accept offers with lower valuations of their homes, which

---

[201] *Koning V Germany (1978) 2 EHRR 170*
[202] *Practical law practice notes, J.P.L, 2010,3, 298-309*
[203] *Shemi Esquire, The Rich Have Lawyers, The London Takings, 2020.*
Shemi Esquire, The compatibility of compulsory purchase orders with human rights,2019; Shemi Esquire, Human Rights and Housing Estate Regeneration, 2020.

[204] *Stars and Chambers v Procurator-where appointment of a temporary sheriff was held to be incompatible with Art 6. One local authority proposed to appoint its own mechanisms of final arbitration.*
[205] *See DCLG guidance; https://www.gov.uk/government/publications/compulsory-purchase-process-and-the-crichel-down-rules-guidance*
[206]*John Spencer, Maureen Spencer, Human Rights Nutcases,2 May 2002*
[207] *https://www.echr.coe.int/documents/guide_art_6_eng.pdf file:///T:/002-7866.pdf*
[208] *Dispossession the great social housing swindle: https://www.dispossessionfilm.com; Shemi Esquire, The Rich Have Lawyers, The London Takings, 2020.*
Shemi Esquire, The compatibility of compulsory purchase orders with human rights,2019; Shemi Esquire, Human Rights and Housing Estate Regeneration, 2020

would otherwise be unacceptable.[209] While for other non-leaseholder tenants, the protracted nature of the housing estate expropriation creates insecurity and disruption.[210]

Imbalance of power and unfair proceedings

During CPO process, there is a manifest imbalance of power, appearance of conflicts of interest in planning processes, a lack of fairness, equality of arms and procedural propriety.[211] Arguably, in local authorities' planning committees, scrutiny committees and cabinet deliberations, decisions are more inclined to favour the interest of the acquiring parties, especially if it is the same local authority.

Residents are accorded less time to present their case or rebut disputable claims presented by the public authorities, which are also the legal acquiring authorities. The cumulative impact of these procedural imbalances is the overall detrimental impact that results into evictions and displacement. A state of affairs that would be consistently incompatible with Art 6 as held in *Borgers v Belgium,*[212] where a defendant who could not hear or make responses, to official arguments, was said to

---

[209] *Stuart Hodkinson, Chris Essen, (2015) "Grounding accumulation by dispossession in everyday life: The unjust geographies of urban regeneration under the Private Finance Initiative", International Journal of Law in the Built Environment, Vol. 7 Issue: 1, pp.72-91, https://doi.org/10.1108/IJLBE-01-2014-0007*

[210] *Shemi Esquire, The compatibility of compulsory purchase orders with human rights, 2019*

Shemi Esquire, Human Rights and Housing Estate Regeneration, 2020; Shemi Esquire, The Rich Have Lawyers: The London Takings , 2020;

[211] *R v (Wright v SOS for health and another (2009) UKHL 3*

[212] *Borgers v Belgium (1993) 15 EHRR 92*

have had his Art 6 rights breached.[213] Another issue that is applicable to art 6 and relevant to CPO processes, is access to information. This is discussed in detail below.

Access to information

Accessibility to material information and the need to be heard is critical to equality of arms.[214] For parties in the process of challenging or asserting their rights, accessing information from public authorities is critical. This could take the form of freedom of information restrictions or subject access data requests. However, freedom of information requests, are protracted affairs and substantial information is not timely provided[215], not provided at all, [216]deducted or is in vague language that does not provide the key details necessary for residents to challenge the CPO. Worse, access to hearings in public is not always guaranteed.[217]

Lack of independent reviews

Apart from the abysmal access to key information, planning functions or processes conducted by local authorities, [218]appear to be more political despite being buttressed by statutory grounds. [219] However, objections do not require a hearing, per

---

[213] *Practical law practice notes public sector.; Shemi Esquire, The compatibility of compulsory purchase orders with human rights, 2019*

Shemi Esquire, Human Rights and Housing Estate Regeneration, 2020; Shemi Esquire, The Rich Have Lawyers: The London Takings , 2020;

[214] *Feldbrugge V Netherlands (1986) 8 EHRR 425, see practice note above.*
[215] *https://www.whatdotheyknow.com/request/asbestos_enquiry#incoming-1327131*
[216] *https://www.whatdotheyknow.com/request/somerleyton_road_steering_group_2321`11*
[217] *Kensington-councillor-DEFENDS-decision-meet-secret.html , https://www.dailymail.co.uk/news/article-4656656/*
[218] *Bryan V UK (1995) 21 EHRR 342*
[219] *DCLG guidance*

se.[220] Therefore, there is a need for a fair balance of rights and access to an independent and impartial decision maker.

An issue that was discussed, in *Tsfayo v UK (2007) ECHR 656*. The key issue involved a claimants' application for *housing and council tax* which was rejected by the review board. The ECHR found that the particular entity was not an *impartial tribunal,* and the possibility of judicial review was not a reprieve from the lack of independence and included councillors.

It is notable that in practice, public authorities who are also the acquiring authorities, review their decisions by committees often staffed by local councillors. Such a situation could imply a lack of a fair and impartial consideration that engages Art 6.

As a minimum, the imminent loss of a home, [221]under art 6, *ought to be given sound, fair and impartial consideration*. Art 6 highlights procedural measures and safeguards to protect parties' convention rights, [222]with emphasis on the protection of residents' legitimate interests.[223] Furthermore, there is a need[224]for objectors to *'have a fair crack of the whip'* by transparent access to pertinent material[225] and be able to have an occasion to dissect evidence meaningfully.[226]

---

[220] R (Adlard V SOS for environment (2002) EWCA
[221] (Ivanova and Cherkezov v. Bulgaria)
[222] (Irina Smirnova v. Ukraine, § 94).
[223] (Orlić v. Croatia, § 64; Gladysheva v. Russia, §§ 94-95; Kryvitska and Kryvitskyy v. Ukraine, § 50; Andrey Medvedev v. Russia, § 55)
[224] Peter Harrison Qc, Glimpsed views of the legal land scape,
[225] R (on the application of Vieira) v Camden LBC
[226] R (on the application of Ashley) Secretary of state for communities and local government

The local planning process is regarded as favourable to developers[227] and the right of appeal is limited to only applicants, although third parties can appeal to the inspector or pursue judicial review. In some cases, there are preconditions placed on valuation processes, which extinguish residents' rights without the legality of the mechanism or action being ascertained, by an impartial tribunal, was held to breach Article 8.[228]

Moreover, where environmental or nuisance complaints are raised, some local authorities, with confidential s106 agreements with developers, may have their impartiality or practical ability to enforce any planning regulations affected. Potentially leading to planning conditions being ignored after grant of planning permission.[229]

Overall, it is evident that planning policies, by the acquiring authorities, who also tend to be the decision makers, in the case of local authorities, prima facie, infringe the rights of enjoyment of property, contain restrictions on legal challenges and may detrimentally affect market value. This would feasibly be a contravention of Art 6 due to a lack of an unbiased, impartial and fair process.

Equal treatment

---

[227] https://www.theguardian.com/cities/2015/jun/25/london-developers-viability-planning-affordable-social-housing-regeneration-oliver-wainwright

[228] '(Kay and Others v. the United Kingdom, § 74).;
Shemi Esquire, The compatibility of compulsory purchase orders with human rights, 2019; Shemi Esquire, Human Rights and Housing Estate Regeneration, 2020.

[229]   https://www.theguardian.com/cities/2019/mar/25/too-poor-to-play-children-in-social-housing-blocked-from-communal-playground

Shemi Esquire

Article 14 has no free-standing existence in absence of other rights. Equality[230] and fairness of treatment under estate regeneration can be pursued in conjunction with Art 8,as was the case in *Karner,* where a breach of Art 14,was found, when an *'occupant was prohibited from succeeding a tenancy after the death of his same-sex partner.'*[231]

Art 14 also covers racial discrimination and was held to amount to a type of degrading treatment under Art 3. This was reiterated in the treaty of Rome as a free standing equal-treatment guarantee, although the UK did not sign that treaty.

The race audit and the institute of race relations,[232]have investigated and reported, racial disparity in housing in general, which is exacerbated by the consequential displacement of housing estate expropriation. The displacement is worsened by discrimination or unfair treatment in valuations and racially disproportionate outcomes of estate regeneration.[233]

Furthermore, under art 14, local authorities, ought to be fully cognizant of the address the particular *'needs'* of minorities and those with protected characteristics. That protection might include imposing certain conditions within certain limits.[234] For

---

[230] *https://www.echr.coe.int/*

[231] *(Karner v. Austria, §§ 41-43; Kozak v. Poland, § 99).*
[232] *JESSICA PERERA, The London Clearances: Race, Housing and Policing, 2019 Shemi Esquire, The Rich Have Lawyers, The London Takings, 2020;*
Shemi Esquire, The compatibility of compulsory purchase orders with human rights,2019; Shemi Esquire, Human Rights and Housing Estate Regeneration, 2020;

[233] *https://www.ethnicity-facts-figures.service.gov.uk/*
[234] *(Connors v. the United Kingdom, § 84) (Chapman v. the*

United Kingdom [GC], § 96; Yordanova and Others v. Bulgaria, §§ 129-130 /(Codona v. the United Kingdom

instance, in *Chapman,* the court affirmed that restricting the use of caravans, has an impact on the applicants respect for their home.

Since estate regeneration imposes restriction on the use, ownership and disposal of property, the ruling in *Chapman,* would be consistent with residents affected by estate regeneration, who may be disadvantaged by the displacement and dispossession associated with estate expropriation.[235]

As mentioned above, racial minorities [236] face a disproportionate detrimental impact[237]in housing and during estate expropriation. As such, this would appear to be incompatible with the judgment in *Larkos v. Cyprus,* where the court held that offering differential protection to tenants against eviction, according to whether they are renting state-owned property, or renting from private landlords, entailed a violation of Article 14, in conjunction with Article 8, *'due to the unjustifiable difference of treatment.'*[238]

Discrimination or racial disparity in CPOs is legislated for, beyond the ECHR and the HRA 1998. Other applicable international conventions bar discrimination and extend a moral authority, [239] which is given legal effect by *the international convention on civil and political rights.*[240] Under these conventions, the articles applicable to housing are articles *23, 22, 3, 14, and 26, inter alia, ratified by the UK in 1976.*[241] As well as the

---

[235] *(Chapman v. the United Kingdom [GC], § 73).*

[236] *just-space-response-to-panel-note-7.3-20-may-2019.pdf, https://justspacelondon.files.wordpress.com/2019/04*

[237]*JESSICA PERERA, The London Clearances: Race, Housing and Policing, 2019*

[238] *Shemi Esquire, The Rich Have Lawyers, The London Takings, 2020;*
Shemi Esquire, The compatibility of compulsory purchase orders with human rights,2019; Shemi Esquire, Human Rights and Housing Estate Regeneration, 2020;

[239] *http://www.un.org/en/universal-declaration-human-rights/*

[240] *https://www.ohchr.org/en/professionalinterest/pages/ccpr.aspx*

[241] *our-human-rights-work/monitoring-and-promoting-un-treaties, https://www.equalityhumanrights.com/*

harmful discriminatory effect, the detrimental impact of housing measures associated with CPOs, can have an impact on individual and community health. Both of which are recognised under international law.[242]

However, the availability of such avenues under the international conventions, does not equate to practical legal relief for those impacted by discriminatory treatment including in the context of estate regeneration. It would appear, despite the ratification by member states such as the united kingdom, that the international conventions such as those mentioned above, can provide an added layer or a modicum of moral as well as diplomatic pressure rather than a tangible mechanism of legal relief, for ordinary citizens affected by CPOs.[243]

Remedial Measures under Art 14

The cardinal remedial principle appears to be, that states are encouraged to implement adequate protections with[244] a positive obligation for a member state to cultivate appropriate safeguards. A Lack of legal capacity, dispossession without

---

[242] *Thiele, Bret. "The human right to adequate housing: a tool for promoting and protecting individual and community health." American Journal of Public Health 92.5 (2002): 712-715.; Shemi Esquire, The Rich Have Lawyers, The London Takings, 2020;*
Shemi Esquire, The compatibility of compulsory purchase orders with human rights, 2019; Shemi Esquire, Human Rights and Housing Estate Regeneration, 2020;

[243] *Ponder, Emily. "Gentrification and the right to housing: How hip becomes a human rights violation." Sw. J. Int'l L. 22 (2016): 359.*
[244] *(Stenegry and Adam v. France (Dec.)).*

meaningful participation in the process and a lack of access to the final determination by the courts, was found to be a violation of art 8, having considered protection measures in national state law.

This was further emphasised in the Supreme Court,[245] to the effect that the Equality Act 2010, provided further protection to a group of people who fall under the protected characteristics category. There are also additional requirements under the public sector duty of the EA2010, in respect of CPOs, as highlighted below.

Public Sector Education Duty[246]

Under S149 of EA2010, *'a public authority must, in the exercise of its functions, have due regard to the need to—eliminate discrimination, harassment, victimisation and any other conduct that is prohibited by or under this Act .*

The act also calls for the ' *advance equality of opportunity between persons who share a relevant protected characteristic and persons who do not share it; foster good relations between persons who share a relevant protected characteristic and persons who do not share the need to—tackle prejudice and promote understanding. Compliance with the duties in this section may involve treating some persons more*

---

[245] *In Akerman –Livingston v Aster Communities Ltd (UKSC) 15,*
;Shemi Esquire, The compatibility of compulsory purchase orders with human rights, 2019

Shemi Esquire, Human Rights and Housing Estate Regeneration, 2020; Shemi Esquire, The Rich Have Lawyers: The London Takings , 2020;
; Equality Act 2010 (legislation.gov.uk)[246] *Public sector equality duty, EA2010*

favourably than others; but that is not to be taken as permitting conduct that would otherwise be prohibited by or under this Act. [247]

In practical terms, the public sector duty, in the context of estate regeneration, can be measured among other means, through the equality impact assessments. However, just like in almost other keys stages, the process tends to be driven by local authorities, which are also the acquiring authorities pushing for CPOs which in turn drive residents from their homes. The basic integrity of the process and outcomes is not only questionable, but potentially meaningless, in terms of seeking meaningful redress for impacted racial minorities, in areas like Lambeth, Southwark, Lewisham, among other boroughs in London.[248]

The correct and fair process would arguably involve an independent professional process that would have the trust of residents and effect genuine remedial measures to mitigate the racial impact of the estate regeneration. In the absence of such measures, it is difficult to ascertain any meaningful steps taken by local authorities, to legally implement the public sector education duty.[249]

---

[247] *Shemi Esquire, The compatibility of compulsory purchase orders with human rights, 2019*

Shemi Esquire, Human Rights and Housing Estate Regeneration, 2020; Shemi Esquire, The Rich Have Lawyers: The London Takings , 2020;

[248] *Shemi Esquire, The Rich Have Lawyers, The London Takings, 2020;*
Shemi Esquire, The compatibility of compulsory purchase orders with human rights, 2019; Shemi Esquire, Human Rights and Housing Estate Regeneration, 2020;

[249] *Shemi Esquire, The Rich Have Lawyers, The London Takings, 2020;*
Shemi Esquire, The compatibility of compulsory purchase orders with human rights, 2019; Shemi Esquire, Human Rights and Housing Estate Regeneration, 2020;

Besides, Art 8, 6 and 14 of the ECHR, A1P1 plays a key role in the CPO process. It is also arguably one of the most prominent article, associated with property rights,[250] under ECHR, as discussed in detail below.

Article 1 of the first protocol- ECHR[251]

Scope

A1P1 protects a landowner's property interests and rights with limitations. A1P1 states that, *'every natural person or legal person is entitled to the peaceful enjoyment of his possessions, and no one shall be deprived of his possessions except in the public interest and subject to the conditions provided for by law and by the general principles of international law. The preceding provisions shall not, however, in any way, impair the right of a state to enforce such laws as it deems necessary to control the use of property in accordance with the general interest or to secure the payment of taxes or other contributions or penalties.*[252]

Art A1P1,[253]covers all forms of property and does not limit ownership of possessions such as physical goods and is independent of national state definitions. However, it does not cover prospective possessions or future possessions but emphasises current possessions.

A landowner's *legitimate expectation* of enjoyment of property rights can be a basis for asserting A1P1, as held in *Pine Valley Developments,* where the applicant had

---

[250] *Ploeger, Hendrik D., and Daniëlle A. Groetelaers. "The importance of the fundamental right to property for the practice of planning: An introduction to the case law of the European Court of Human Rights on Article 1, Protocol 1." European Planning Studies 15.10 (2007): 1423-1438.*
[251] *Referred to here as A1P1.*
[252] *Guide_Art_1_Protocol_1_ENG.pdf, https://echr.coe.int/Documents/*
[253] *See Practical Law UK practice Note 8-385 5732.*

bought land under the expectation of planning permission being approved. This could be applicable to estate regeneration due to expectations of the legal security of their property interests, leases and secure tenancies whose curtailment would engage A1P1.[254]

The expectation of legal security was mirrored, in *Stretch*[255]*,* where an *'applicant complained that he had been unjustly denied extension of a further 21-year term lease',*[256] and the choice allowed by the local authority had been' *ultra vires'.*[257] The court ruled that *'having regard to those considerations, there was a disproportionate interference with the applicant's peaceful enjoyment of his possessions and therefore, concludes that there has been a violation of Article 1 of Protocol No. 1 to the Convention'*[258]*.* Therefore, the curtailment of resident's leases or secure agreements, during estate regeneration could engage A1P1.[259]

In *Plant v Lambeth, the* court held that A1P1 had not been engaged in respect of secure tenants' rights. However, a potential legal claim under A1P1 should merit consideration as a possession or asset, where a property-owner has a lawful belief, that such a claim can be decided by a court.[260] These decisions are applicable to property expropriation affected parties, who have diametrically opposed interests with

---

[254] *Pine developments v Ireland (1992) 14 EHRR 319*
[255] *Stretch v UK (Application no. 44277/98)*
[256] *Practical Law UK practice Note 8-385 5732.*
[257] *Practical Law UK practice Note 8-385 5732.*
[258] *Stretch v UK (Application no. 44277/98)*
[259] *Shemi Esquire, The Rich Have Lawyers, The London Takings, 2020;*
Shemi Esquire, The compatibility of compulsory purchase orders with human rights,2019; Shemi Esquire, Human Rights and Housing Estate Regeneration, 2020;

[260] *Pressos Compani Naviera v Belgium (1995) 2 EHHR 3010), also see Practical Law UK practice note 8-385 5732.*

the acquiring authorities, who are also the local key decision makers in all facets of the CPO trigger process.[261]

Justification

Under A1P1, dispossessing someone of their property can only be warranted in extraordinary situations. There ought to be sufficient proximity to '*market value*' of the property although the applicant needs to prove '*deprivation,*' not *mere restrictions,*[262] or temporary deprivation of use or enjoyment.' As an example, in *Lithgow et al,* deprivation of property was held to have happened where the state confiscated property by way of a CPO.

In *Sporrong and Lonnroth*, the *expropriation of building permits and building restrictions* enforcement, for specific durations was held to be interference in the applicants' enjoyment of their land, amounting to deprivation of property.[263]

Even a partial loss of a significant or substantial part of a landowner's right, can lead to deprivation without full expropriation. This principle is consistent with housing estate expropriation affected residents facing significant restrictions, such as construction hazards like noise, fumes, vibration or contaminants or the restriction to sell.[264]

---

[261] *Shemi Esquire, The Rich Have Lawyers, The London Takings, 2020;*
Shemi Esquire, The compatibility of compulsory purchase orders with human rights, 2019; Shemi Esquire, Human Rights and Housing Estate Regeneration, 2020;

[262] *See Practical Law UK practice Note 8-385 5732.*
[263] *Sporrong and Lonnroth (1982)5 EHHR 35*
[264] *Imrie, R., & Thomas, H. (1997). Law, Legal Struggles and Urban Regeneration: Rethinking the Relationships. Urban Studies, 34(9), 1401–1418. https://doi.org/10.1080/0042098975484*

In *James v UK,*[265] the court found that individuals with leases under the leasehold reform Act 1967, who were entitled to long leases but could purchase freeholds of their leases, at a defined statutory price, deprived freeholder of their property, due to the inability to sell the property or set the sale price.[266]

Paradoxically, this can benefit housing estate expropriation affected residents[267] to disentangle them from the acquiring authority, although the acquiring authority would still have significant statutory powers to initiate a CPO, by citing other grounds such as control. However, seizure or forfeiture, in certain cases, would not be deemed deprivation. This was the issue in *Agosi V UK,*[268] where the issue was *'seizure and forfeiture by customs of smuggled Kruegerrands.'*[269]

Furthermore, there is need to balance community interests and safeguarding of a person's right to a *peaceful enjoyment* of their property, to rationalize the use of property in the public interest. In practice, however, this affords significant latitude for acquiring authorities to use this as a defence in CPOs.[270]

Market value

There could be violation where applicants are prevented from selling their properties at market value. Such interference appears disproportionate since compensation

---

[265] *James V UK (1986) 8 EHRR 123*
[266] *See Practical Law UK practice Note 8-385 5732.*
[267] *See Cressigham Gardens in Lambeth*
[268] *Agosi v UK (1987) 9 EHRR1*
[269] *Practical Law UK practice Note 8-385 5732.*
[270] *See R Plant V LLBC (cite full)*

should be *reasonably related to the market value.* However, A1P1 does not guarantee a *'right to full compensation'* in every situation since a *'margin of appreciation'* is permitted to the local authorities in this respect.[271]

However, as highlighted by *Justice Scalia in Kelo*, the issue is beyond 'market value' per se, *since market rate,* in this context is disputed and described as 'a euphemism for imposing compensation' on an unwilling seller[272]. Where owners are compelled to sell to a specific party, at a specific time, at a price largely determined by the same interested party who is also possibly the acquiring authority and arbiter of the planning decisions, a manifest conflict of interest.[273]

Typically, residents buy properties without any CPO in mind, with leases usually for 125 years. They envisaged this as a safety net both as a home and capital accumulation. In areas like London, where the land values rise significantly, this is a natural attraction for developers. *The 'no scheme'* principle is unrealistic since CPO affected areas face blight and disrepair which affect the market price.[274] Therefore, the application of market price or resemblance to market price does not reflect the just, fair and equitable compensation for residents and their families.[275]

---

[271] *See Lithgow and Practical Law UK Practice Note 8-385 5732*

[272] *Guy Roots et al, 2ⁿᵈ edition*

[273] *Neil Gray Libby Porter, By Any Means Necessary: Urban Regeneration and the "State of Exception" in Glasgow's Commonwealth Games 2014*

[274] *Loretta Lees, Mara Ferreri, resisting gentrification on its final frontiers: Learning from the Heygate Estate in London (1974–2013), Cities, Volume 57,2016, Pages 14-24, https://doi.org/10.1016/j.cities.2015.12.005.(http://www.sciencedirect.com; Shemi Esquire, The Rich Have Lawyers, The London Takings, 2020;*
Shemi Esquire, The compatibility of compulsory purchase orders with human rights,2019; Shemi Esquire, Human Rights and Housing Estate Regeneration, 2020;

[275] *Shemi Esquire, The Rich Have Lawyers, The London Takings, 2020;*
Shemi Esquire, The compatibility of compulsory purchase orders with human rights,2019; Shemi Esquire, Human Rights and Housing Estate Regeneration, 2020;

Besides market price, under A1P1, compensation is also a relevant measure in assessing the balance or the proportionate nature of the burden on any CPO affected party.[276]*In James v UK* and in *the former king of Greece et al v Greece*[277], it was held that compensation that does not *reasonably* reflect the value of the property[278] could be deemed a *'disproportionate interference'*.[279]

The central concern for *'compulsorily purchased landowners,'* is stated to be *'timely adequate compensation.'* [280] The central issue here was the *'limitation period'* *associated* with compensation.

The concern above, emphasises, the expeditious nature and *'totality of compensation'* as central to amicable resolutions of CPO disputes. Acquiring authorities seek to offer less compensation through a deliberately slow process, while peoples' lives are on hold pending compensation.[281]

Acquiring authorities should avoid being unconscionable[282]and employ ADR.[283] Since litigation remains a protracted, expensive and unpredictable process.[284]

---

[276] *Deborah Rook, Property and Human Rights, 2001*
[277] *Deborah Rook, Property Law and Human Rights, 2001*
[278] *Deborah Rook, Property Law and Human rights, 2001*
[279] *Holy Monasteries v Greece*
[280] *Saunders V Caerphilly CBC (2015) EWHC 1632 CH;*
[281] *Alice Belotti, Estate regeneration and Community impact, LSE, 2016; Shemi Esquire, Human Rights and Housing Estate Regeneration, 2020*
[282] *John Pugh –Smith, when is' enough 'legally enough, Encyclopaedia of Local government law bulletin,2015, Citing Saunders V Caerphilly CBC (2015) EWHC 1632 CH*
[283] *Alternative dispute resolution*
[284] *Ridgeland properties Ltd V Bristol city council (2011) EWCA civ 649 ;(2011) R.V.R 232; (2011)5 WLUK 827 (CA) Civ Div.)*

This was demonstrated in a case where the court overturned *the 'value of the scheme found to be £1.25millons more than the baseline scheme'.*[285] Clearly significantly affecting the losing parties.[286]

Proportionality

Under A1P1, *proportionality* accentuates a reasonable equilibrium between the public *interest and the property interests of the owners.*[287] State authorities enjoy a *'wide margin of appreciation'* in determining *'the public or community interests, within the law'*[288] by reflecting a need to be *'accessible, precise and foreseeable'.*[289]

Other aspects determining fair balance encompass procedural safeguards of owner's property rights, the nature of the penalty applied,[290] the extent of interference, *'duration,'*[291] the fault, its significance and the *'irrationality or arbitrary nature'* of the statute.[292] For concerned residents, proportionality in *'control cases '* is not a basis for compensation but indicates a *'need for a fair balance to be found.'* The interference may only be *'justified legally in the general interest.'*[293]

---

[285] *Richard Harwood, J.P.L 2011,11,1498-1517*
[286] *Shemi Esquire, The Rich Have Lawyers, The London Takings, 2020;*
Shemi Esquire, The compatibility of compulsory purchase orders with human rights,2019; Shemi Esquire, Human Rights and Housing Estate Regeneration, 2020;

[287] *See James V UK App No 8793/79 (A/98) (Official Case No)*
[1986] ECHR 2 (Neutral Citation); James and ors v United Kingdom, Decision on Merits, App no 8793/79, B/81, 11th May 1984, European Commission on Human Rights (historical) [ECHR]
[288] *Practical Law UK practice Note 8-835 57.*
[289] *Hentrich V France (1994 18 EHRR 440 (1994) ECHR 29 Lithgow,*
[290] *International Transport Roth v HS (2002) EWCA Civ 158*
[291] *Sporrong and Lonnroth*
[292] *R(Kensall) v SOS for Environment (2003) Admin 2003*
[293] *See Practical Law UK practice Note 8-385 5732.*

States are further allowed a margin of appreciation, in implementation of decisions, associated with legitimate objectives of public interest considerations[294] applicable to measures designed to *'achieve greater social justice.'* In Tesco Stores Ltd v SOS[295] for Environment and Transport (2000), Sullivan J emphasised the need for a *'fair balance to be struck between the public interest'* such as *'redevelopment'* and the *'individual's right to a peaceful and quiet enjoyment of his possessions'.* Adding that, such interference ought to be *'proportionate and necessary'* to meet the *'compelling case in the public interest'* tests which *'reflects the necessary element of that balance'.*[296] In *Chesterfield properties v Secretary of State,*[297]it was noted, that *'only another interest, a public interest, of greater force may override it'* (In a CPO inspector's report,.[298] Objectors argued that as the leaseholders, *article 1 and 8 rights* have been breached, and it is binding upon the *acquiring authority* to justify the infringement in terms of its legal *proportionality* to the violation.[299]

The objectors referred to, *'*R (Clays Lane) v Housing Corporation, where Maurice Kay J stated that *'the appropriate test of proportionality requires a balancing exercise'* Since *'a decision which is justified based on a compelling case in the public interest as being reasonably necessary'* may not be *'obligatorily the least intrusive of Convention rights.'*[300]

---

[294] *James v UK above*

[295] *J.P.L 2010,3 298-309*

[296] *Also see see R (Clays Lane Housing cooperative ltd v Housing corp (2005), R (Pascoe v SOS (2007), R (Hall) v First SOS (2008) J.P.L 63 at 15*

[297] *Chesterfield Properties Plc v Secretary of State for Environment & Ors [1997] EWHC Admin 709 (24th July 1997), http://www.bailii.org/ew/cases/EWHC/Admin/1997/709.html*
Cite as: 76 P & CR 117, (1997) 76 P & CR 117, [1997] EWHC Admin 709

[298] *CPO Report NPCU/CPO/A5840/74092, www.planningportal.gov.uk/planning inspectorate Page 73*

[299] *CPO Report NPCU/CPO/A5840/74092, www.planningportal.gov.uk/planning inspectorate Page 73*

[300] *Indeed some 'leaseholders no longer have mortgages, and many are no longer in employment, because of the CPO they will be separated from their family or friends and will be unable to afford to return to the estate.'*

Shemi Esquire

The inspector agreed based on *'Paragraph 12 of the Guidance'* and concluded that[301] *'the interference with human rights would not be proportionate having regard to the level. The public benefits that the scheme would bring… a compelling case in the public interest has not been proved.'* The case illustrates the argument and lived experiences of residents as highlighted in the examples above. Further emphasising the necessity for human rights to be a fulcrum and not simply a peripheral matter, in CPOs.[302]

Interference

Under the ECHR, tax enforcement could be justification where the A1P! *margin of appreciation,* principle could be applicable. Under this rule, a state *has' a right to implement laws considered essential to regulate use of property in accordance with the public interest to obtain payment of taxes, penalties or laws.* If the power is exercised *'rationally* and *'proportionately,'* such as regulating a sex shop.[303] In *Davies,* the court held that A1P1 was engaged, in the *'absence of fair compensation'* thereby

---

[301] *Further states that an acquiring authority should be sure that the purposes for which the compulsory purchase order is made justify interfering with the human rights of those with an interest in the land affected. They would need to invest considerable personal resources in addition to any compensation they would receive for their properties; the CPO would not only deprive them of their dwelling but also their financial security. If they chose not to pursue this option, they would inevitably need to leave the area and this would have implications for their family life, including the lives of that dependant on the…. together with the failure of the scheme to fully achieve the social, economic and environmental well-being.*

[302] *Shemi Esquire, The compatibility of compulsory purchase orders with human rights, 2019*

Shemi Esquire, The Rich Have Lawyers, The London Takings, 2020;
Shemi Esquire, The compatibility of compulsory purchase orders with human rights,2019; Shemi Esquire, Human Rights and Housing Estate Regeneration, 2020;

[303] *Belfast CC v Miss Behavin' Ltd, ([2007] WLR 1420, [2007] 1 WLR 1420, [2007] 3 All ER 1007, [2007] UKHL 19, http://www.bailii.org/uk/cases/UKHL/2007/19.html*

breaching the need for striking a 'fair balance' between the public interest and the *'van owners'*. However, there was a *'wide margin of appreciation,'* since the council had an *'appeal system, regarded as 'reasonable' and proportionate.'*

The court could also find a breach, where there is a discretionary or unfair procedure creating an excessive burden born by the applicant and can further intervene in the absence of a reasonable justification for interference with property rights.[304] Affirming that natural or legal persons can only be deprived of property, subject to conditions provided by law and the *'general principles of international law'* or other interests,[305] such as *'contributory or non-contributory'* state benefits.[306]

It is also arguable that the fair practice would be to offset any outstanding payments as part of the compensation, since complaints or appeals may depend on residents' securing evidence from acquiring authorities. What is clear is that any Interference must be proportionate, with a constructive responsibility on member states to ensure proportionality with the stated aim. However, despite the statutory obligations, there are doubts about local authorities' willingness to enforce their own statutory liability or culpability. Hence necessitating a need for Art 8 intervention, where there are unfit conditions but no adequate remedy.[307]

CPOs, right to buy and A1P1

[304] *R Mott v Environment Agency (2018) UKSC 10)*
[305] *Beyeler v Italy (2001) 33 EHRR 52*
[306] *Stec v UK (2005)41 EHRR SE18*
[307] *HA1985 s604,*

R Plant v LLBC[308] highlights issues facing secure tenants subjected to a CPO and interference in their right to buy under A1P1. A central issue was whether A1P1 was engaged and breached by the council's decision. The court stated that A1P1 was not pertinent to the council's cabinet decision, concluding that, *'A1P1 is not engaged and indistinguishable from other authorities.*[309] Which the claimant alleged to have been breached due to interference with S118 of HA 1985, right to buy and S84 (1) rights, which prevent the court from issuing a possession order on such a property. Except on legal grounds in schedule 2 of the Act and other provisional requirements.[310] Noting that 'if *engaged, it need only be considered in relation to the statutory right to buy when the authority commences County Court proceedings to obtain an order for possession of a particular home'.*[311]

The court appeared to restrict this to the fact that the claimant had not already exercised his right to buy. However, the existence of that option and its removal appeared to interfere in the claimant's property rights, engaging A1P1.[312]

Nevertheless, the court appeared to acknowledge that A1P1 was engaged to the point when steps would be taken to revoke it. Stating that, *'If, contrary to the clear view I have reached, I had concluded that A1P1 was engaged in LLBC's decision, reached*

---

[308] *R Plant v LLBC, [2016] EWHC 3324 (Admin)*

[309] *Kay v Lambeth LBC [2005] QB 352 and Austin v Southwark LBC [2010] HLR 1'.*

[310] *R Plant v LLB [2016] EWHC 3324 (Admin)*

[311] *Shemi Esquire, The Rich Have Lawyers, The London Takings, 2020;*
Shemi Esquire, The compatibility of compulsory purchase orders with human rights, 2019; Shemi Esquire, Human Rights and Housing Estate Regeneration, 2020;

[312] *Shemi Esquire, The Rich Have Lawyers, The London Takings, 2020;*
Shemi Esquire, The compatibility of compulsory purchase orders with human rights, 2019; Shemi Esquire, Human Rights and Housing Estate Regeneration, 2020;

on 21 March 2016…. the issue of whether it was breached would have been a matter for the Court to determine.'[313] Inviting the question as to when the right time or forum would be for the claimant to enforce his rights under A1P1.

For CPO affected secure tenants, the court appears to have acknowledged their rights if they chose to move away. They would be deemed to be secure tenants provided with new secure tenancies if they decide to move elsewhere, but not if they wish to be rehoused in a new home on their current location. In which case they would only be granted an assured tenancy. For leaseholders, suitable compensation that allows them to stay in the locality is key.[314]

Compensation

Compensation is set by statute equating to[315] market value plus home loss payments with disbursements,[316] disregarding, *the value of the scheme'* on the value of the land[317]. However, this equation does not cover the detrimental effects of being displaced from a settled community and the spiral effects.[318]

---

[313] *Citing Belfast City Council v Miss Behavin' Ltd [2007] 1 WLR 1420 at paragraphs 13 to 15)'.*

[314] *Shemi Esquire, The Rich Have Lawyers, The London Takings, 2020;*
Shemi Esquire, The compatibility of compulsory purchase orders with human rights, 2019; Shemi Esquire, Human Rights and Housing Estate Regeneration, 2020;

[315]*compulsory-purchase-process-and-the-crichel-down-rules-guidance*
https://www.gov.uk/government/publications
[316]*https://assets.publishing.service.gov.uk/government*
[317] *Compensation payable for the compulsory acquisition of an interest in land is based on the 'equivalence principle' (i.e., that the owner should be paid neither less nor more than their loss).'[317]*
[318] *Martine August, "It's all about power and you have none:" The marginalization of tenant resistance to mixed-income social housing redevelopment in Toronto, Canada,*
Cities, Volume 57, 2016, Pages 25-32, (http://www.sciencedirect.com

Shemi Esquire

Compensation assumes a willing seller without compulsion via monetary payment. This is at the public *'market value* 'of the land, *in so far as money can do it,' to put one in the same position as land had not been taken from him, in so far as loss imposed on him in the public interest, but no greater.'*[319]

Although under A1P1, compensation could be paid,[320] the legitimate public interest may *'justify less than the financial equivalent to what the claimant lost',* based on the principle in *James.*[321] Similarly, *'where rights to compensation are provided by statute'*, those *'provisions* must be interpreted in compatibility with HRA 1998'.[322]

However, A1P1 does not state how much compensation should be paid but states that *'the taking of property without any just compensation is justifiable only in exceptional circumstances'*[323]. It is arguable, compensation should be beyond pecuniary loss as summed up by Justice Scalia in *Kelo.*[324] *Justice Scalia* notes that, *'yes you are paying for it, but you are giving the money to somebody, who does not want the money, who wants to live in the house that she's lived in her whole life. That counts for nothing. 'What this lady wants is not money. No amount of money is going to satisfy her. Living in this house her whole life. She does not want to move.'*

---

[319] *Lord justice Scott in Horn v Sunderland corporation; A government review culminated into law commission reports that were not implemented*[319] *leading to minimal changes.*[319]
[320] *Guy Roots et al, 2nd edition*
[321] *James V UK, The Law of compulsory purchase, third edition, Guy Roots et al; Thomas v Bridgend county council, (2011), EWCA Civ 862, (2011) RVR 241*
[322] *Such as in Thomas v Bridgend county council, (2011), EWCA Civ 862, (2011) RVR 241, where the CA held that s19(3) of the Highway Act 1980, was incompatible with art 1 of the ECHR.*
[323] *Guide_Art_1_Protocol_1_ENG.pdf, https://echr.coe.int/Documents*
[324] *Kelo v. City of New London, 268 Conn. 1, 843 A.2d 500, 843 A. 500 (2004).*

Shemi Esquire

The *Kelo case*, highlights the sense of deep injustice of the compulsory taking of homes in situ, especially where there is no tangible or proven compelling public interest.[325]

Beyond monetary compensation

As part of restitution, occupiers should be, without means-testing, entitled to rehousing[326] under liberal criterion., because they have been displaced.[327]

For many residents affected by estate expropriation, especially those with young children, finding secure and affordable accommodation is one of the most formidable barriers. Many are compelled to live on potentially hazardous and dangerous protracted construction sites, such as asbestos contaminated land, move into temporary accommodation. Others are forced to move out of the locality, which debatably triggers a series of detrimental impact in their lives.[328] Therefore, during CPOs, rehousing and compensation remain a key remedial step to minimising the impact of displacement, largely left to local authorities.

---

[325] *Kelo v. City of New London, 268 Conn. 1, 843 A.2d 500, 843 A. 500 (2004).*
[326] *s.39 (1) Land Compensation Act 1973, as amended by para 6, Sch.15 Housing Act 2004*
[327] *R v East Hertfordshire District Council ex p Smith (1990) 23 HLR 26; R v Bristol Corporation ex p Hendy [1974] 1 WLR 498.*
[328]*PaulWatts,Its_not_for_us_Regeneration_the_2012_Olympics_and_the_gentrification_of_East_London_City_2013, http://www.academia.edu/6007431/;;Shemi Esquire, The compatibility of compulsory purchase orders with human rights, 2019*

Shemi Esquire, Human Rights and Housing Estate Regeneration, 2020; Shemi Esquire, The Rich Have Lawyers: The London Takings , 2020;

Zoe Williams, the real cost of regeneration,http://www.execreview.com/2017/07/the-real-cost-of-regeneration/

Although, A1P1 refers to principles of international law,[329] as   reflected by the ICCPR, [330] ICESCR, [331] CERD /ICE [332] and CROC, [333] enforceability and legal jurisdiction remain a hurdle.[334] Therefore, compensation via this route remains a largely academic issue. In the event of a breach of the above, residents have to consider the possibilities of remedial measures. Below the potential legal remedies are discussed below.[335]

Remedies

Article 41[336]

Article 41 refers to what is termed as *'just satisfaction'*, to a successful claimant, whose rights have been violated, a causal link between loss and violation, including speedier proceedings that could have a better life outcome.[337]

---

[329] *Egon Scweb, The Protection of the Right of Property of Nationals under the First Protocol to the European Convention on Human Rights, The American Journal of Comparative Law*
Vol. 13, No. 4 (Autumn, 1964), pp. 518-541
[330]*International convention on civil and political rights, https://www.ohchr.org/EN/ProfessionalInterest/Pages/CCPR.aspx*
[331] *International convention on social and economic rights, https://www.ohchr.org/en/professionalinterest/pages/cescr.aspx*
[332] *Committee on elimination of racial discrimination, https://www.ohchr.org/en/hrbodies/cerd/pages/cerdindex.aspx*
[333] *Convention on the right of a Child, https://www.ohchr.org/EN/ProfessionalInterest/Pages/CRC.aspx*
[334] *It is therefore difficult to envisage this as a practical immediate relief to residents affected by CPOs, because it would require implementation by the faulting nation states through protracted legal and political mechanisms.*

[335] *Shemi Esquire, The Rich Have Lawyers, The London Takings, 2020;*
Shemi Esquire, The compatibility of compulsory purchase orders with human rights, 2019; Shemi Esquire, Human Rights and Housing Estate Regeneration, 2020;

[336] *article-41, https://www.coe.int*
[337] *Convention_ENG.pdf, https://www.echr.coe.int/Documents/*

It states among other provisions, that, *'If the court finds a violation of the convention or the protocols... and the internal law of the high contracting party concerned allows only partial reparation to be made, the court shall, if necessary, afford just satisfaction to the injured party.'*[338]

Under article 41, compensation is awarded for what is classified as *'pecuniary damage, non –pecuniary damage, costs* and *expenses,'* placing the applicant in the position they were in, but for the violation, termed as *'restitution in integrum.'* That is, actual loss ('damnum emergens'), 'diminished gain,' future loss (*'lucrum cessans').*[339]

However, the practical application of art 41 by estate regeneration affected parties remains questionable for all the reasons discussed above, such access to resources among other encumbrances. However, it may act as reference point and a deterrence in negotiations with the acquiring parties to focus on expeditious resolution and just compensation.[340]

Further relief

Other potential legal remedies include *negligence, deceit or actionable misstatement.* Proceedings can be initiated at the appropriate court or tribunal. Under Government

---

[338] *article-41, https://www.coe.int*
[339] *article-41, https://www.coe.int;*
[340] *Shemi Esquire, The Rich Have Lawyers, The London Takings, 2020;*
Shemi Esquire, The compatibility of compulsory purchase orders with human rights,2019; Shemi Esquire, Human Rights and Housing Estate Regeneration, 2020;

guidance[341] further relief can be sought through statutory prescription under s.234 (4)

198, before expiry of six weeks after vesting.[342]

Additionally, *'estoppel or legitimate expectation,* 'could be another option for

consideration, by CPO affected applicants. It would appear without demonstration of

the 'public interest,' estoppel, could be argued by the claimants as relief.[343] Other relief

could also be where states can also issue measures like payments as appropriate,

reopening of proceedings, changes to legislation and discontinuation of

proceedings.[344] But neither Art 13 nor the convention in general, appear to require

contradicting states to implement provisions of convention in any particular manner.[345]

Damages under HRA are subject to a limitation period in tandem with Art 6 and are

not recoverable as of right, except, in accordance with the principle of just satisfaction,

in exceptional circumstances.[346] In that context, it appears that art 41 also remains an

unpractical option for CPO affected residents. There is therefore a need for practical

remedial mechanisms associated with human rights breaches linked to CPOs, to

---

[341] *https://www.gov.uk/government/publications/compulsory-purchase-process-and-the-crichel-down-rules-guidance*
[342] *J.P.L 2010,5 552-556*
[343] *Alec Samuels, The planning process and judicial control: the case for better judicial involvement and control, J.P.L 1570*
[344] *Mowbray, A. (2002). Duties of Investigation under the European Convention on Human Rights. International and Comparative Law Quarterly, 51(2), 437-448. doi:10.1093/iclq/51.2.437; Shemi Esquire, The Rich Have Lawyers, The London Takings, 2020; Shemi Esquire, The compatibility of compulsory purchase orders with human rights,2019; Shemi Esquire, Human Rights and housing Estate Regeneration, 2020;*

[345]*Shemi Esquire, The Rich Have Lawyers, The London Takings, 2020; Shemi Esquire, The compatibility of compulsory purchase orders with human rights,2019; Shemi Esquire, Human Rights and Housing Estate Regeneration, 2020;*

;

[346] *JUST SPACE / JUST SPACE ECONOMY AND PLANNING GROUP A response to the Mayor's document A City for All Londoners 11 December 2016*

mitigate the detrimental impact,[347] although this could, require legislative as well as regulatory reform.[348]

International law [349]

A1P1 refers to principles of international law[350] and in the case of property rights perhaps more reflected by the ICCPR. [351] These instruments are aimed at protecting economic, social, political rights of individuals or groups; however, enforceability and legal jurisdiction remain a hurdle.[352] While the international law framework, regards housing as a fundamental need, a human right, the courts within the ECHR jurisdiction, appear to look at this in terms of respect for a home and enjoyment of one's possession. It would appear the international legal standards appears more legally suitable to the plight of residents faced with estate expropriation, than simply referring to respect for a home, as the benchmark. It is a weak tick the box approach, which is indefensible in one of the wealthiest, economic blocks in the world.[353] Simply put, what

---

[347] *SEE planning commission suggestion insert in reforms Alec Samuels, The planning process and judicial control: the case for better judicial involvement and control, J.P.L 2007, 1570-1577*
[348] *Shemi Esquire, The Rich Have Lawyers, The London Takings, 2020;*
Shemi Esquire, The compatibility of compulsory purchase orders with human rights, 2019; Shemi Esquire, Human Rights and Housing Estate Regeneration, 2020;

[349] *https://www.ohchr.org; Shemi Esquire, The Rich Have Lawyers, The London Takings, 2020;*
Shemi Esquire, The compatibility of compulsory purchase orders with human rights, 2019; Shemi Esquire, Human Rights and Housing Estate Regeneration, 2020;

[350] *Egon Scweb, The Protection of the Right of Property of Nationals under the First Protocol to the European Convention on Human Rights, The American Journal of Comparative Law*
Vol. 13, No. 4 (Autumn, 1964), pp. 518-541
[351] *International convention on civil and political rights, https://www.ohchr.org/EN/ProfessionalInterest/Pages/CCPR.aspx*
[352] *It is therefore difficult to envisage this as a practical immediate relief to residents affected by CPOs, because it would require implementation by the faulting nation states through protracted legal and political mechanisms.; Shemi Esquire, The compatibility of compulsory purchase orders with human rights, 2019*

Shemi Esquire, Human Rights and Housing Estate Regeneration, 2020; Shemi Esquire, The Rich Have Lawyers: The London Takings , 2020;

[353] *EU-position-in-world-trade, https://ec.europa.eu/trade/policy.*

does it say about a society that is unable to guarantee shelter, both *de jure and de facto,* to its population, especially the most vulnerable.

The ECHR, legal framework should amend and afford guaranteed legal protection to impacted residents, instead of focusing on strained points associated with respect for *a home* and enjoyment *of possessions*. These are arguably vaguely construed standards that are commingled with other procedural safeguards, as opposed to entrenched tangible rights that are categorically protected by law. The current approach is consistent with arguably legally ineffective measures, with unaffordable cost encumbrances for residents and varying standards of *'margins of appreciation,'* akin to a get out of jail card for local authorities, engaged in estate expropriation.[354]

In a nut-shell, ECHR, as an arguable living instrument, ought to implement, the legal standard of a right to a home as a basic need[355]. International law stipulates a right to adequate housing[356] that requires concrete legal protection.[357] As argued, since housing is intertwined with health, education, employment, family and community, among other fundamental needs, it should attract a more stringent, non-adversarial

---

[354] *Reform, E. C. H. R. "Margin of Appreciation." An overview of the Strasbourg Court's margin of appreciation doctrine. URL: https://www. opensocietyfoundations. org/sites/default/files/echrreform-margin-of-appreciation. pdf (дата обращения: 29.10. 2016) (2012).*

[355] *Letsas, George. "The ECHR as a living instrument: Its meaning and legitimacy." Constituting Europe: The European Court of Human Rights in a National, European and Global Context 2 (2013): 106.*

[356] *Thiele, Bret. "The human right to adequate housing: a tool for promoting and protecting individual and community health." American Journal of Public Health 92.5 (2002): 712-715.*

[357] *Hohmann, Jessie. The right to housing: Law, concepts, possibilities. Bloomsbury Publishing, 2013. Leckie, Scott. From housing needs to housing rights: An analysis of the right to adequate housing under international human rights law. London: International Institute for Environment and Development, 1992.; Shemi Esquire, The compatibility of compulsory purchase orders with human rights, 2019*

Shemi Esquire, Human Rights and Housing Estate Regeneration, 2020; Shemi Esquire, The Rich Have Lawyers: The London Takings , 2020;

and concrete legal protection. As opposed to a focus on nuanced legal standards such as enjoyment of possession or a respect for a home under the ECHR.[358]

Proposals for reform

Estate expropriation impacts and has a causal link to an amalgamation of macro and micro economic, social and political factors. Central governments through budgetary brief, influence local spending priorities. In that respect, housing is bound to be impacted either through spending, legislation or planning directives. In London, the local mayor, has powers over planning and funding.[359] Despite central government power, local authorities still have a considerable influence over the final decision, in terms of what and when to expropriate as well as planning decisions.[360]

Therefore, in the first instance, reform should incorporate central government increase of spending on housing, amending national legislation to restrict wholesale demolition of homes and maintain a level of direct control.

Although the Secretary of state has a say in the CPO process, it remains ineffective and is more tangible at the end of the process, when many residents have already

---

[358] *Calzolari, Valentina, and Jonathan Barnes. "The Right To Housing Under The Echr." Human Rights as Indivisible Rights. Brill Nijhoff, 2009. 113-148.; Shemi Esquire, The compatibility of compulsory purchase orders with human rights, 2019*

Shemi Esquire, Human Rights and Housing Estate Regeneration, 2020; Shemi Esquire, The Rich Have Lawyers: The London Takings , 2020;

[359] *, Sadiq Khan withdraws cash from Lambeth estate projects,*
Sadiq Khan withdraws cash from Lambeth estate projects (architectsjournal.co.uk), 7th October 2020
[360] *Shemi Esquire, The Rich Have Lawyers, The London Takings, 2020;*
Shemi Esquire, The compatibility of compulsory purchase orders with human rights, 2019; Shemi Esquire, Human Rights and Housing Estate Regeneration, 2020;

been displaced[361]. In effect, by the time the decision reaches the secretary of state, events on the ground already have influenced the outcome as was indicated in the Aylesbury decision.[362]

In terms of local government, there needs to be a more practical and tangible inter partisan and public involvement at all levels. At a decision-making level, a departure from a majority cabinet system to a consensus based multi-partisan approach, would arguably stem the dominance of single political parties at local levels, where there are single party voter loyalty tendencies.

In the case of London, for example, labour tends to dominate local and central government elections, which then leads to complacency, incompetence and in some cases arguable impunity. A pattern that can be cured by a community based and multiparty agency approach.[363] For instance, in Haringey, a combination of a community-based campaign, legal action and voter revolt led to the extensive, Haringey estate expropriation being abandoned, as the labour party was forced to listen to residents.[364]

---

[361] *Shemi Esquire, The Rich Have Lawyers, The London Takings, 2020;*
Shemi Esquire, The compatibility of compulsory purchase orders with human rights, 2019; Shemi Esquire, Human Rights and Housing Estate Regeneration, 2020;

[362] *Romyn, Michael. "New Deal? Aylesbury Regenerated, 1997–2010." London's Aylesbury Estate. Palgrave Macmillan, Cham, 2020. 225-274; Aylesbury Estate, https://www.london.gov.uk/what-we-do/planning/planning-applications-and-decisions/planning-application-search/aylesbury-estate-*

[363] *Allmendinger, Phil, and Graham Haughton. "Post-political spatial planning in England: a crisis of consensus?" Transactions of the Institute of British Geographers 37.1 (2012): 89-103.; Degen, Mónica, and Marisol García. "The transformation of the 'Barcelona model': an analysis of culture, urban regeneration and governance." International journal of urban and regional research 36.5 (2012): 1022-1038.; Gaventa, John. "Representation, community leadership and participation: citizen involvement in neighbourhood renewal and local governance." Report, Neighbourhood Renewal Unit, Office of Deputy Prime Minister, July 04. (2004).; Shemi Esquire, The compatibility of compulsory purchase orders with human rights, 2019*

Shemi Esquire, Human Rights and Housing Estate Regeneration, 2020; Shemi Esquire, The Rich Have Lawyers: The London Takings , 2020;

[364] *Minton, Anna. "The price of regeneration." Places Journal (2018).; Dillon, Denis, and Bryan Fanning. Lessons for the Big Society: planning, regeneration and the politics of community participation. Routledge, 2016; Smyth, Stewart. "Reforms and resistance: how tenants can influence housing policy." British Politics and Policy at LSE (2018); Russell, Bertie, and Keir Milburn.*

Shemi Esquire

A synopsis of other proposals for reform includes community land trusts,[365] codified legal protection of residents,[366] refurbishment,[367] instituting independent entities that concentrate on the assessment of life outcomes, especially children, equitable compensation and expeditious rehousing among other proposals.[368]

In relation to the renovation option, a pattern has emerged, where local authorities have pivoted to demolition rather than refurbishment or infill among other potential options. In the absence of any plausible explanation, this raises questions about the real intention of regeneration. If indeed social housing is the genuine priority, that is the legal rationale for CPOs, then the instinctive priority should be on refurbishment and utilisation of other commercial spaces, as opposed to demolition of existing homes as the first step.[369]

In fact, as some cases have shown, what appear to be reasonable objections have been rejected by the courts. These include alternatives to regeneration, provision of accommodation and residents led development. The refusal by the courts of what

---

"Neoliberals wanted to transform the institutions of economic and social life so that they demand individuals behave as individualistic self-maximisers. The left now needs to commit to the commoning of our institutions so that they engender collective and solidaristic behaviour."; Shemi Esquire, The Rich Have Lawyers, The London Takings, 2020;
Shemi Esquire, The compatibility of compulsory purchase orders with human rights, 2019; Shemi Esquire, Human Rights and Housing Estate Regeneration, 2020;

[365] *Brett Christophers, The New Enclosures, the Appropriation of Public Land in Neoliberal Britain*
[366] *Stuart Hodkinson (2011) The Private Finance Initiative in English Council Housing Regeneration: A Privatisation too Far? Housing Studies, 26:6, 911-932, DOI: 10.1080/02673037.2011.593133*
; mill wall-the-den-cpo-scheme-Lewisham-council.
https://www.theguardian.com/football/2017/jan/24
[367] *Crawford, Kate, et al. "Demolition or Refurbishment of Social Housing? A review of the evidence." (2014).*
[368] *Health Impact Assessment, edited by John Kemm, Jayne Parry, Stephen Palmer, Stephen R. Palmer; Shemi Esquire, The compatibility of compulsory purchase orders with human rights, 2019 Shemi Esquire, The Rich Have Lawyers, The London Takings, 2020;*
Shemi Esquire, The compatibility of compulsory purchase orders with human rights, 2019; Shemi Esquire, Human Rights and Housing Estate Regeneration, 2020;

[369] *Crawford, Kate, et al. "Demolition or Refurbishment of Social Housing? A review of the evidence." (2014).*

would appear to be reasonable objections, raises the legal bar high, in terms of what residents need to demonstrate to challenge the CPO evictions successfully.[370]

Therefore, there is an urgent need for legislation and courts to mandate that CPOs are only used as a last resort and only in a demonstrably clear, with practically tangible, beneficial interest to the affected communities that can morally and legally equate to the displacement of entire communities.[371] The legal standard should not simply be a peripheral academic reference to an abstract futuristic public interest that may not materialise in practice but then results in displacement.[372]

Other measures point to the empowerment of residents who live on the housing estates. For example, in London, after intense pressure, a ballot requirement was made a prerequisite to the mayor's funding for regeneration. However, local councils such as Lambeth appear to have circumnavigated the requirement by stating that it will not seek the mayor's funding. Among the various proposals for reform, perhaps the key measures that could stem the avalanche of estate expropriation that results in displacement and other detriments to residents, is the legally enforceable requirement for a ballot by residents. This would ideally be effective where the local authority cannot circumnavigate the ballot without a court order.[373]

---

[370] *Judicial review of compulsory purchase order decisions - Shelter England*

[371] *Shemi Esquire, The Rich Have Lawyers, The London Takings, 2020;*
Shemi Esquire, The compatibility of compulsory purchase orders with human rights, 2019; Shemi Esquire, Human Rights and Housing Estate Regeneration, 2020;

[372] *Cooper, Adam Elliott, Phil Hubbard, and Loretta Lees. "Sold out? The right-to-buy gentrification and working-class displacements in London." The Sociological Review 68.6 (2020): 1354-1369.*

[373] *Lambeth estate 'regeneration' in doubt after Sadiq Khan pulls funding on four projects because Council refuses to ballot tenants – Brixton Buzz*

Furthermore, there is a need for a legal imperative for refurbishment to be the first viable measure based on sound structural expert evidence. However, evidence appears to indicate that in several areas, after millions of funds were spent, there is little correlation to genuine social housing built that was the basis of the legal rationale for home expropriation.[374]

As another reform measure, compensation should be legally aligned with the value of buying a similar property, in the existing locality, considering the change of circumstances, age, current or future earning potential and other relevant factors that may inhibit or affect residents to secure mortgages. Especially that residents had no difficulties meeting their current mortgage payments but for the estate regeneration[375].

In addition, CPO shared ownerships schemes should be replaced with a quid pro quo approach, by enacting a home for home, quid-pro-quo exchange.[376] This would relieve residents from being compelled to place a substantial amount of their house equity and compensation into more costly new homes of the same or smaller size in the same location.[377]

---

[374] Watt, Paul. "Displacement and estate demolition: multi-scalar place attachment among relocated social housing residents in London." Housing Studies (2020): 1-24.
[375] Shemi Esquire, The compatibility of compulsory purchase orders with human rights, 2019

Shemi Esquire, Human Rights and Housing Estate Regeneration, 2020; Shemi Esquire, The Rich Have Lawyers: The London Takings , 2020;

[376]Richardson V Midland Heart; https://www.theguardian.com/housing-network/hidden-dangers-shared-ownership
[377] Shemi Esquire, The compatibility of compulsory purchase orders with human rights, 2019

Shemi Esquire, Human Rights and Housing Estate Regeneration, 2020; Shemi Esquire, The Rich Have Lawyers: The London Takings , 2020;

Finally, rehousing as a guarantee of affected should be a prerequisite prior to any construction or demolition taking place. Once construction commences, residents are compelled, under duress, to move or are displaced, to protect their health and wellbeing. This lessens the pressure and legal urgency of the local authority to rehouse residents, leading to multiple spiral detrimental impacts. It is important to note that these proposals are not exhaustive nevertheless, a synopsis of some of these proposals above provides a scope for such a detailed analysis.[378]

Conclusion

This analysis explored the legal requirements, justification, processes, impact and the compatibility of human rights with estate regeneration through CPOs.[379] The historical context paints a pattern of privatisation of public land over the long-term, in which CPOs are just part of the weapons[380] that legitimise property acquisition in estate expropriation.[381] During the process, the choices appear onerous for residents. Essentially, residents must choose between demolition of homes without meaningful involvement or acquiesce to gross interference in their lives and displacement.[382] Leading to an emerging theme of the prospect of estate expropriation appearing incompatible with human rights.[383] Such incompatibility seems to be manifested through procedural or substantive unfair processes characterised with adverse

---

[378]*Briefly, the central themes suggest improvement of consultation, transparency, scrutiny of financial viability or funding claims, rigorous assessment of social or affordable housing, protection of residents' health and safety, access to legal independent free advice, rehousing as well as a fair expeditious and independent process.*

[379] *Phil Hubbard & Loretta Lees (2018) The right to community? City, 22:1, 8-25, DOI: 10.1080/13604813.2018.1432178*
[380] *Brett Christophers, The New Enclosures, the Appropriation of Public Land in Neoliberal Brit*
[381] *Jessica Perera, London clearances, Race, Housing and policing, http://www.irr.org.uk*
[382] *Phil Hubbard & Loretta Lees (2018) The right to community? City, 22:1, 8-25, DOI: 10.1080/13604813.2018.1432178*
[383] *Sarah Nield (2013) Article 8 Respect for the Home: A Human Property Right? King's Law Journal, 24:2, 147-171, DOI: 10.5235/09615768.24.2.147*

outcomes.[384] A situation that highlights the need for human rights protections to be treated as legally fundamental and enforced during the estate expropriation process.[385]

A failure to implement and enforce human rights protections, risks regarding the ECHR,[386] HRA[387] or international instruments,[388]as merely academic, inconsequential overstated antidotes, akin to domesticated lions or paper tigers.[389] This could create circumstances that can lead to a total abdication of human rights to the whims and primal instincts of profit focused entities, with the potential complicity of acquiring authorities.[390] A free for all or winner takes it all approach, which arguably places communities' well-being, at the mercy of opaque financial practices [391] with unaccountable planning authorities.[392]

The evolving potential consequences could similarly shape outcomes that shake the very fabric of a fair democratic, progressive society, in which one's property and inherent intrinsic corresponding rights are deemed protected by law. Where expropriation takes place, it ought to be through a judicially fair and equitably

---

[384] *ethnic-inequalities-London-capital-all*
https://www.trustforlondon.org.uk
[385] *Javid-rejects-Aylesbury-estate-cpo-as-breach-of-human-rights,https://www.architectsjournal.co.uk*

[386] *Kenna, P. (2008). Housing rights: positive duties and enforceable rights at the European Court of Human Rights. European Human Rights Law Review, 13(2), 193-208*
[387] *Kenna, P. (2008). Housing rights: positive duties and enforceable rights at the European Court of Human Rights. European Human Rights Law Review, 13(2), 193-208*
[388] *https://www.ohchr.org/en/professionalinterest/pages/cescr.aspx*
[389] *Douglas Maxwell, Journal of planning & Environmental Law, Article 1 of the First protocol: A paper tiger in the face of compulsory purchase orders for private profit?*
[390] *Peter Newman ' Ian Smith' Cultural production, place and politics on the South Bank of the Thames, First published: 28 June 2008.*
[391] *Jerry Flynn (2016) Complete control, City, 20:2, 278-286, DOI: 10.1080/13604813.2016.1143685*
[392] *London-council-aylesbury-estate-development-southwark-financial-risk, https://www.theguardian.com; Shemi Esquire, The compatibility of compulsory purchase orders with human rights, 2019*

Shemi Esquire, Human Rights and Housing Estate Regeneration, 2020; Shemi Esquire, The Rich Have Lawyers: The London Takings , 2020;

compensated process, in strict tandem with the public interest or public good, beyond the fig leaf of so-called imposed market rate.

Since societies are reportedly judged by how they treat the weakest in society,[393] there is an obvious need for human rights protection to be a fundamental tenet in this area. *After all human rights should be universal[394] as well as erga omnes.[395]* Although this stipulation is emphasised by Art 1 and 2 of UDHR, It remains to be seen how the ECHR, is practically beneficial for communities in situ, in current and future CPO implementations.[396]

The courts should interpret the act in a manner that reflects the arguable intergenerational severity of the detrimental impact, associated with de-homing and displacement. Where there is proven impact on health and wellbeing, associated with, for example, hazardous construction elements, the courts should be able to unambiguously protect residents, compensate them and punish offenders. Proving the public interest, should be a stringent legal test that an acquiring party should prove in tandem with the harmful outcome.[397]

Above all, compensation should be reformed to reflect the wider damage caused, by mandating the totality of circumstances, as part of the human rights regime not just a

---

[393] *Attributed to Ghandi et al.*

[394] *https://www.un.org/en/universal-declaration-human-rights/*

[395] *Kadelbach, S. (2006). "Chapter II. Jus Cogens, Obligations Erga Omnes and Other Rules - the Identification of Fundamental Norms". In the Fundamental Rules of the International Legal Order. Boston, USA: Brill | Nijhoff. doi: https://doi.org/10.1163/ej.9789004149816.i-472.10*

[396] *The articles state that' ,inter alia, All human beings are born free and equal in dignity and rights. They are endowed with reason and conscience and should act towards one another in a spirit of brotherhood. 'Everyone is entitled to all the rights and freedoms set forth in this Declaration, without distinction of any kind, such as race, colour, sex, language, religion, political or other opinion, national or social origin, property, birth or other status. Furthermore, no distinction shall be made based on the political, jurisdictional or international status of the country or territory to which a person belongs, whether it be independent, trust, non-self-governing or under any other limitation of sovereignty.'[396]*

[397] *Shemi Esquire, The compatibility of compulsory purchase orders with human rights, 2019*

Shemi Esquire, Human Rights and Housing Estate Regeneration, 2020; Shemi Esquire, The Rich Have Lawyers: The London Takings , 2020;

statutory   requirement. A failure to do that could put in peril genuinely publicly

beneficial projects and social housing due to strong opposition from the affected

parties, communities and the wider public. A daunting but avoidable prospect if human

rights were practically central to housing estate expropriation schemes.[398] Perhaps the

first step is to avoid treating the current CPO regime, as a sacred cow that is beyond

reform or criticism, but one that demonstrates the credentials of the envisaged *living*

legal instrument that adopts to contemporary challenges with corresponding legal

remedies.[399]

Bibliography

1.   MHCLG: Guidance on compulsory purchase process and the Crichel down

Rules for the disposal of surplus land acquired by, or under the threat of, compulsion;

https://www.gov.uk/government/publications/compulsory-purchase-process-and-the-

crichel-down-rules-guidance.

2.   The Implications of Kilo in Land Use Law, Symposium Articles: Keynote

Address - Kelo, Lingle, and San Remo Hotel, Santa Clara Law Review, Vol. 46, Issue

4 (2006), pp. 787-810 Curtin, Daniel J. Jr

---

[398] *Shemi Esquire, The Rich Have Lawyers, The London Takings, 2020;*
Shemi Esquire, The compatibility of compulsory purchase orders with human rights, 2019; Shemi Esquire, Human Rights and Housing Estate Regeneration, 2020;

[399] *Yuwen, F. A. N. Revisiting ECtHR Interpretation of the ECHR: Living Up to a Living Instrument. Vol. 65. Torkel Opsahl Academic EPublisher, 2016.; Letsas, George. "The ECHR as a living instrument: Its meaning and legitimacy." Constituting Europe: The European Court of Human Rights in a National, European and Global Context 2 (2013): 106.; Theil, Stefan. "Is the 'living instrument' approach of the European Court of Human Rights compatible with the ECHR and International Law?." European Public Law 23.3 (2017).*

3.   Globalization, Communities and Human Rights: Community-Based Property Rights and Prior Informed Consent,2006 Sutton Colloquium Article, Denver Journal of International Law and Policy, Vol. 35, Issue 3 & 4 (Summer-Fall 2007), pp. 413 428 https://heinonline.org/419

4.   Human Rights and Property Rights [article] United States Law Review, Vol. 64, Issue 11 (November 1930), pp. 581-594 Blume, Fred H.

5.   Equating Human Rights and Property Rights--The Need for Moral Judgement in an Economic Analysis of Law and Social Policy, Ohio State Law Journal, Vol. 47, Issue 1 (1986), pp. 163-200 Malloy, Robin Paul

6.   Douglas Maxwell, Journal of planning & Environmental Law, Article 1 of the First protocol: A paper tiger in the face of compulsory purchase orders for private profit?

7.   Towards   a   Compulsory   Purchase   Code: https://www.lawcom.gov.uk/project/towards-a-compulsory-purchase-code/

8.   Compulsory acquisition of land: Developers, by PLC Property https://uk.practicallaw.thomsonreuters.com

9.   Planning Act 2016: http://www.housing.org.uk/resource-library/browse/the-housing-and- planning-act-2016/

10.   Kept in the Dark; https://www.transparency.org.uk

11.   The Law of compulsory purchase, third edition, Guy Roots et al

12.   Estate-regeneration-why-people-power-is-forcing-london-to-rethink-housing; developers-alarmed-at-khans-plans-to-give-estate-residents-power; https://www.architectsjournal.co.uk/news

13.   Mayor-and-conservatives-dispute-latest-London-housing-stats; https://www.insidehousing.co.uk

14.   Phil Hubbard, Loretta Lees. (2018) the right to community? *City* 22:1, pages 8-25.

15.   Faulty-towers;

https://www.transparency.org.uk/sites/default/files/pdf/publications, Aug 2017 pdf

16.   Shemi Esquire, The Rich Have Lawyers, The London Takings, 2020;

17.   Shemi Esquire, The compatibility of compulsory purchase orders with human rights,2019;

18.   Shemi Esquire, **Human Rights and Housing Estate Regeneration,** 2020;

19.   Towards a paradigm of Southern urbanism Seth Schindler City Volume 21, 2017 - Issue 1Published online: 6 Mar 2017

20.   Reconstructing Berlin: Materiality and meaning in the symbolic politics of urban space

21.   Dominik Bartmanski et al. City Volume 22, 2018 - Issue 2 Published online: 17 Apr 2018.

22.   Editorial Editor-in-Chief's note: What/whose order is to be asserted in the city?

23.   Bob Catterall City Volume 22, 2018 - Issue 2

24.   Published online: 7 Jun 2018.

25.   The right to community?: Legal geographies of resistance on London's gentrification frontiers

26.   Phil Hubbard et al. City Volume 22, 2018 - Issue 1 Published online: 15 Mar 2018 editorial.

27.   Editorial: The right to assert the order of things in the city Luke R. Barnesmoore City

28.   Volume 22, 2018 - Issue 2 Published online: 7 Jun 2018.

29.   Stuart Hodkinson, Chris Essen, (2015) "Grounding accumulation by dispossession in everyday life: The unjust geographies of urban regeneration under the Private Finance Initiative", International Journal of Law in the Built Environment, Vol. 7 Issue: 1, pp.72-91, https://doi.org/10.1108/IJLBE-01-2014-0007

30.   Towards a new perspective on the role of the city in social movements: Urban Policy after the 'Arab Spring' Raffael Beier City Volume 22, 2018 - Issue 2 Published online: 17 Apr 2018.

31.   Adonis, A., and B. Davies, eds. 2015. City Villages: More Homes, Better Communities. London: IPPR., https://www.ippr.org/publications/city-villages-more-homes-better-communities

32.   The London Borough of Southwark (Aylesbury Estate Site 1B-1C) Compulsory Purchase Order 2014 ('the Order': http://35percent.org/img/Decision_Letter_Final.pdf

33.   Prime minister pledges to transform sink estates, https://www.gov.uk/government/news/prime-minister-pledges-to-transform-sink-estates: 10 January 2016.

34.   'Cameron time to demolish sink estates', https://www.bbc.co.uk/news/av/uk-politics-35275516/cameron-time-to-demolish-worst-sink-housing-estates, 10 January 2016.

35.   Compulsory purchase and Compensation: An Overview of the system in England and Wales, By Frances Plimmer.

36.   Paul Watt & Anna Minton (2016) London's housing crisis and its activisms, City, 20:2, 204-221, https://doi.org/10.1080/13604813.2016.1151707

37.   Participation in the right of access to adequate housing, 14 Tulsa J Comp. & Intl L 269 2006 -2007, Hein online

38.   Republic of SA v Grootboom & others 2000(11) BCLR 1169

39.   Evadne Grant, Enforcing Social and Economic Rights: The right to adequate housing in south Africa, 15 Afr, J, intl & Comp, L 1 (2007), Hein online

40.   The requirements for a compelling case in the public interest to justify a CPO (High Court) by Practical Law Planning: In Horada v Secretary of State for Communities and Local Government [2015] EWHC 2512 (Admin), Volume: 25 issue: 1, page(s): 115-135

41.   The privatization of council housing, Norman Ginsburg, Issue published: February 1, 2005, https://doi.org/10.1177%2F0261018305048970

42.   Haringey Council votes to cancel development vehicle despite Lendlease warning 18 July 2018, https://www.insidehousing.co.uk/news/news/haringey-council-votes-to-cancel-development-vehicle-despite-lendlease-warning-57250:

43.   Watt, P. 2015. "The IMD as a WMD in the Regeneration of London Council Estates: Tackling Spatial Inequalities and Producing Socio-spatial Injustice." Paper at Tackling Spatial Inequalities Conference, Sheffield, September 10

44.   Paul Watt (2009) Housing Stock Transfers, Regeneration and State-Led Gentrification in London, Urban Policy and Research, 27:3, 229-242, https://doi.org/10.1080/08111140903154147

45.   Pam Douglas & Joanne Parkes (2016) 'Regeneration' and 'consultation' at a Lambeth council estate, City, 20:2, 287-291, https://doi.org/10.1080/13604813.2016.1143683

46.   Bracking V Secretary of state for works and pensions [2013] EWCA Civ 1345, [2014] Eq LR 60

47.   Knock it down or Do it UP?, The challenge of estate regeneration https://www.london.gov.uk/about-us/london-assembly/london-assembly-publications/knock-it-down-or-do-it

48. HPA 2016 and how it affects housing associations, http://www.lag.org.uk/magazine/2016/07/a-devastating-blow-to-social-housing-in-england.aspx.

49. EA2010Equality Act 2010 (Specific Duties and Public Authorities) Regulations 2017. PSED: specific duties in England, Practical Law UK Practice Note

50. CPA 1965: Compulsory Purchase Act 1965.

51. CP (VD) A 1981: Compulsory Purchase (Vesting Declarations) Act 1981.

52. LCA 1961: Land Compensation Act 1961.

53. LCA 1973: Land Compensation Act 1973.

54. TCPA 1990: Town and Country Planning Act 1990

55. https://www.libertyhumanrights.org.uk/

56. https://www.equalityhumanrights.com/en/about-us

57. https://www.ohchr.org/en/professionalinterest/pages/ccpr.aspx

58. https://echr.coe.int/

59. British Institute of human rights www.Bihr.org.uk

60. Chartered Institute of Housing www. Cih.org

61. DCLG www.coommunites.gov.uk

62. Housing Law practitioners Association www. Hipa.org.uk

63. The Law Society www.lawsociety.org

64. https://savecressingham.wordpress.com/

65. Cressingham-gardens-regeneration-approved-in-high-court, http://www.insidehousing.co.uk

66. http://35percent.org/2013-06-08-the-heygate-diaspora

67. https://www.southwarknews.co.uk/news/council-given-permission-take-aylesbury-estate-cpo-case-high-court-disappointing-blow-campaigners/

68.   http://www.shelter.org.uk

69.   http://www.axethehousingact.org.uk/page/2/ on

70.   Localism Act 2011, https://uk.practicallaw.thomsonreuters.com/1-504-2706

71.   Housing and equality law, By Robert Brown, Arden Chambers

a.   https://uk.practicallaw.thomsonreuters.com/w-012-0034

72.   Compulsory-purchase-life-after-aylesbury,   https://www.ashurst.com/en/news-and-insights/legal-updates

73.   https://www.birketts.co.uk/insights/legal-updates/compulsory-purchase-and-what-to-do-about-it

74.   https://assets.publishing.service.gov.uk/government/uploads/system/uplods/attachment_data/file/551698/ECHR_Memorandum.pdf

75.   Alternative-development-proposals-how-do-they-affect-cpo-validity, https://www.burges-salmon.com/news-and-insight/legal-updates

76.   Housing and Regeneration Act 2008, Housing and Regeneration Act 2008

a.   http://www.opsi.gov.uk/acts/acts2008/ukpga_20080017_en_1

77.   Donnelly, Jack. Universal human rights in theory and practice. Cornell University Press, 2013.

78.   Human rights Act 1998: https://uk.practicallaw.thomsonreuters.com/0-506-9287

79.   Dealing with a human rights challenge,https://www.lexisnexis.com/uk/lexis psl/publicl

80.   New law journal: https://www.newlawjournal.co.uk

81.   Practicallaw: https://uk.practicallaw.thomsonreuters.com, Practice/PublicLaw

82.   Hansard- https://hansard.parliament.uk/

83. Cressingham-Gardens-tenant-wins-High-Court-legal,

https://www.leighday.co.uk, November-2015

84. Labour-council-regeneration-housing-crisis-high-court-judge,

https://www.theguardian.com/commentisfree/2017/oct/25

85. The Secretary of states' ruling re: Town and Country Planning Act 1990 Section

226(1) (a), Acquisition of Land Act 1981 The London Borough of Southwark (Aylesbury

Estate Site 1B-1C) Compulsory Purchase Order 2014 ('

86. https://hsfnotes.com/realestatedevelopment/2016/09/28/a-new-right-to-a-

community-decision-by-the-secretary-of-state-not-to-confirm-the-cpo-for-aylesbury-

estate/

87. Compulsory_purchase_process_and_the_Crichel_Down_Rules_-

_guidance_updated_180228;

88. https://assets.publishing.service.gov.uk/government/uploads/system/uploads/

attachment_data/file/684529/

89. http://www.legislation.gov.uk/ukpga/2010/15

90. Legal-updates,the-neighbourhood-planning-act-2017/,https://www.burges-

salmon.com/news-and-insight

91. Section149, https://www.legislation.gov.uk/ukpga, 2010

92. https://assets.publishing.service.gov.uk/government/uploads/system/uploads/

attachment_data/file/475271/cpo_guidance.pdf

93. Knock It Down or Do It Up,

https://www.london.gov.uk/sites/default/files/gla_migrate_files_destination/

94. London's Housing Crisis Worse for Ethnic Minorities 22 March 2016;

https://www.runnymedetrust.org

95. Dispossession the great social housing swindle: https://www.dispossessionfilm.com/

96. City Villages, More Homes, Better communities: https://www.ippr.org/files/publications/pdf/city-villages_Mar2015.pdf

97. Shelter. 2015. Homes for our Children. How much of the Housing Market is Affordable? https://england.shelter.org.uk/Homes_for_our_Children.pdf

98. The-story-of-the-camberwell-submarine-4618, https://www.insidehousing.co.uk/insight/insight

99. Convention for the Protection of Individuals with regard to Automatic Processing of Personal Data Strasbourg, 28.I.1981 https://rm.coe.int/CoE

100. Legal Challenges to Implementing CPOs and Decisions under the Crichel down Rules by Tim Mould QC, http://www.landmarkchambers.co.uk/userfiles/TM.pdf

101. The use of compulsory purchase powers for regeneration by Elvin QC, http://www.landmarkchambers.co.uk

102. Land Compensation Claims: The Claimants Perspective by Simon Pickles Landmark Chambers, http://www.landmarkchambers.co.uk/cases-compulsory_purchase_compensation.aspx

103. Compulsory purchase orders: stage 4, CPO compensation procedure: flowchart by Practical Law Planning, https://uk.practicallaw.thomsonreuters.com/2-629-7353

104. Twenty years later Assessing the significance of the Human Rights Act 1998 to the residential possession proceedings, By Ian Loveland http://openaccess.city.ac.uk/17163/

105. Housing Act 1988, https://www.legislation.gov.uk/id/ukpga/1988/50

106. R on the application of Sainsbury's supermarket ltd) V Wolverhampton city Council (2010) UKSC

107. Waters v welsh development agency (2004)1WLR 1304

108. David Elvin QC paper, Use of compulsory purchase powers for regeneration, http://www.landmarkchambers.co.uk

109. Countryside Alliance v Attorney General [2007] UKHL 52

110. Article 1 of the first Protocol to the ECHR: protection of property, Practical Law UK Practice Note, https://uk.practicallaw.thomsonreuters.com/8-385-5732

111. Article 6 of the ECHR: right to a fair hearing Housing:

112. https://uk.practicallaw.thomsonreuters.com/2-385-8106

113. Part VII of the Housing Act 1996, https://uk.practicallaw.thomsonreuters.com

114. Demolition or refurbishment of social housing? ,https://www.ucl.ac.uk/engineering-exchange/research-projects/2018/nov/demolition-or-refurbishment-social-housing

115. Stanton, J. (2014). The Big Society and Community Development: Neighbourhood Planning under the Localism Act. Environmental Law Review, 16(4), 262–276.

116. Murungaru v Home Secretary [2008] EWCA Civ 1015

117. Fazia Ali v The United Kingdom - 40378/10 Court (Fourth Section)) [2015] ECHR 924

118. Belfast City Council v Miss Behavin' Ltd [2007] UKHL 19

119. James V UK (A98 (1986 E.H.R.R 123 (ECHR)

120. Sporrong and Lönnroth [1982] 5 EHRR 35

121. Le Compte, Van Leuven and De Meyere v Belgium [1981] ECHR 3.

122.   Bryan v United Kingdom [1995] ECHR 50, (1996) 21 EHRR 342

123.   Begum v London Borough of Tower Hamlets [2003] UKHL 5

124.   Lithgow and others v UK [1986] 8 EHRR 329)

125.   Chapman v. the United Kingdom [GC], § 96.

126.   Yordanova and Others v. Bulgaria, §§ 129-130

127.   Zehentner v. Austria, §§ 63 and 65) / (A.-M.V. v. Finland, §§ 82-84 and 90).

128.   Qazi v Harrow LBC (2003 UKHL 43: (2004) 1 AC 983 (HL)

129.   Salvesen V Riddell (2013) UKSC 22: 2013 SC (U.K.S.C) 236(SC)

130.   López Ostra v. Spain, §§ 56-58,

131.   Moreno Gómez v. Spain, § 61.

132.   Di Sarno and Others v. Italy, § 112).

133.   Hatton and Others v. the United Kingdom [GC], § 96.

134.   Moreno Gómez v. Spain, § 53)

135.   Fadeyeva v. Russia, § 69.

136.   (Asselbourg and Others v. Luxembourg (dec.)).

137.   Martínez and Pino Manzano v. Spain,

138.   (Hardy and Maile v. the United Kingdom

139.   (Hatton and Others v. the United Kingdom [GC]

140.   https://www.facebook.com/Savewestburysw8-804075296314550/

141.   https://twitter.com/savewestburysw8

Analysis Of The Human Rights Impact Of Estate Regeneration In the United Kingdom

Shemi Esquire

Lightning Source UK Ltd.
Milton Keynes UK
UKHW050819100223
416674UK00007B/51

9 781471 669392